EFFECTIVE PARENTING PARTICIPANT WORKBOOK

A Court-Approved Guide to Nurturing Healthy
Relationships and Developing Effective Parenting Skills

Dr. Arleen A. Fuller, Ph.D.

Table of Contents

Introduction

Purpose of This Book

The purpose of this workbook is to empower and enable you to become the best parent possible. No matter the reason you are being asked to use this workbook and go through this training process the goal is to help you as you traverse along your parenting journey.

Unfortunately, there is no approved manual on how to be a "good" parent. We have books that teach us how to cook, drive a car, and a million other things. And while, yes, there are hundreds of books in existence claiming to help you be the "best" parent, no book can promise that, not even this one. The reason children do not come with a manual is that each child and each parent is unique. We are all one-of-kind beings, and no one book is going to give you all the answers; but this workbook and guide are here to help.

Parenting is a deeply personal relationship that is influenced by your experiences growing up, your culture, religion, education, socio-economic status, and the personalities of yourself and your child.

The information included in this book covers the basics of infant, child, and teen development. We will delve into physical and mental development and reflect on your personal experiences that may be coloring your parenting. To get the most out of this manual take the information presented seriously; take time to reflect on the questions posed and answer them honestly, even those that may feel uncomfortable.

In addition to children's physical and mental development, we will cover issues including communication, substance abuse, cooperating with a co-parent, health & safety, definitions of child abuse and neglect, discipline, and social-emotional development.

This workbook cannot replace medical or psychological help from a medical or mental health professional, nor is it intended to. Instead, use this guide as precisely that, a guide to lead you in the right direction and to become a more positive and more productive parent. None of us are perfect parents, and no one has ever been the perfect parent; perfection does not exist.

Showing up is what counts. You may feel the use of this workbook is pointless, or that you don't need it, that going through this book won't change anything, and you may be right. But before you completely write off the experience, give yourself the chance to approach these pages with an open heart and an open mind.

Remember, you are here not only for yourself but for your child as well. Whether or not you became a parent by choice, by accident, through adoption, or the loss of a relative, you are here now, and you owe it to yourself and the child in your care to do the best you possibly can.

So welcome. Welcome to the next step in your journey as a parent. Whether your child is three months, three years, or thirteen, this workbook has something for you.

The Role of the Parent

What is the role of a parent? Depending on your culture, religion, and upbringing, this question can be answered in a myriad of ways. Your immediate response may be that a parent's role is to discipline. Another person may say it is to provide and care. A third response might be that a parent's role is to be the authority and teach respect.

All three answers are correct, as well as about a hundred different responses. When we become parents, we are presented with a helpless being. A newborn human cannot survive without someone else taking care of them. We know that a newborn deer can typically walk within 7 hours of being born, and newly hatched baby sea turtles possess the instinct to crawl their way back to the ocean, but newborn humans are helpless.

The only mechanism a human newborn has to seek help is their cry. Newborns cry to tell us everything; their cry tells us they are hungry, sick, hot, cold, lonely, scared, have a messy diaper, or that they want attention. It is our job as parents to decode those cries and respond appropriately to their needs. Therefore, our first role as a parent is to care for our children and supply their needs.

In modern times many children, and adults, confuse needs and rights with wants and privileges. It is a child's right to be provided with shelter, clothing, food, medical care, and love. A parent's job is to strive to fulfill these needs and rights to the best of their ability. That doesn't mean a parent has to provide a huge mansion to live in, name-brand clothing and shoes, or take their child out to 5-star restaurants, but it does mean there should be a clean and safe home, clean clothing, and nutritious food available.

As our children grow, they rely on adults, particularly their parents or parent figures, for their needs and wants and their education. While instinct creates a curiosity in children to learn and develop, their parents and caregivers foster that development and learning.

Therefore, a parent's second role is that of the child's first teacher. Our children learn language when we speak and read to them, and they learn how to crawl and walk because we encourage them to do so. They learn about numbers, colors, shapes, etc., because of an adult's guidance. And that learning continues well beyond preschool. Children and adolescents need adults to help them navigate the uncertain waters of social skills, sex, anxiety, fear, bullying, pride, failure, and triumph.

As a parent, you are not expected to be a developmental or educational specialist, but the saying, knowledge is power, holds true here. The more you understand about your child's development, needs, psychology, and growth, the more equipped you will be to lead them to success in life.

Remember, the goal is not to become the perfect parent, merely to become the best parent possible. You will play many roles in your journey as a parent but keeping in mind the two primary roles of provider and teacher will immensely benefit both you and your child.

Chapter One
Understanding Milestones

Developmental milestones are the markers by which adults and professionals evaluate a child's growth and development. Each stage of development has specific milestones and markers that pediatricians and early childhood developmental specialists look for to see if a child is developing typically. It is also beneficial for parents to be aware of these milestones as well. Parents spend more time with their children than anyone else; therefore, they have ample opportunities to observe their child's abilities.

It is also important to remember that each child develops at their own pace and that just because your child may fall slightly outside of the typical range does not mean there's anything to be concerned about. One child may walk at 12 months while their sibling may walk at eight months. One child may speak their first word at ten months, while another doesn't speak their first word till 12 months.

If you understand milestones, it helps you as a parent recognize when something might be significantly out of the typical range and if your child is failing to meet several developmental milestones. When you suspect this is the case, you should speak with your child's pediatrician and childcare provider.

Parents need to be aware of developmental milestones to understand what their children can and cannot do at certain ages. When you better understand what your child physically and mentally can accomplish, you can parent them better. You may find it frustrating that your 2-year-old continuously spills their drink at the table. But, when you understand that they may not be developmentally ready to drink out of an open cup and that spills are typical, you will likely be more patient and understanding.

2-4 Months	6-9 Months	1 Year	18 Months	2 Years	3-4 Years	5-6 Years	7-8 Years
Smiles & Coos	Recognizes familiar faces, likes to play	Shy or nervous around strangers	May have tantrums	Is excited to see other children	Takes turns in games	Has friends, wants to please friends	Enjoys peer interactions, friends are important
Looks at Parents	Looks at self in a mirror	Hands you a book to read	Shows affection	Shows more independence	Shows concern for friends	Is aware of real and pretend	Seeks acceptance by peers
Turns head towards sounds	Strings vowels together	Responds to simple requests	Points to things of interest	Plays beside other children	Dresses and Undresses self	Shows increasing independence	Demonstrates more independence
Begins to follow things with eyes	Responds to their name	Uses simple gestures	Says several single words	Knows names of body parts	Separates easily from parents	Speaks clearly	Extensive vocabulary
Can hold head up	Shows curiosity	Says Mama, Dada, or similar words	Shakes head no, says no	Says sentences of 2-4 words	Has short conversations	Tells short stories	Asks a lot of questions.
Cries in different ways to show needs	Rolls over both directions	Puts things in and out of containers	Recognizes everyday objects: cup, spoon, ball	Begins to sort shapes and colors	Does puzzles of 3-6 pieces	Counts to 10 or more, Recognizes most letters	Reads short books and stories,
Reaches for toys	Sit without support	Pulls to stand – may walk	Scribbles with fat crayons	Follows 2-step directions	Turns book pages one at a time	Uses scissors with ease	Can write name and many words.
Babbles and copies sounds	Uses finger to point at things	Bangs things together	Walks, may begin running	Names familiar items in a book	Controlled scribbles	Draws simple pictures	Can think abstractly
Pushes down on legs on a hard surface	Plays peek-a-boo	Makes sounds with tone changes	Drinks from a sippy cup	Kicks a ball, throws a ball overhand	Climbs well	Hops and stands on one foot	Enjoys games of precision
Hold a toy and shake it	Stands holding on	Finds hidden things easily	Eats with a spoon	Walks up and downstairs	Runs easily	Catches a ball	Increased agility & flexibility

Below we have included some typical developmental milestones for birth through age eight. This is by no means a complete and comprehensive list, but it does provide you a general understanding of what is considered the typical development of a young child.

DEVELOPMENTAL MILESTONES BIRTH – EIGHT

The CDC has free checklists you can print and use as an observation tool with your child from the age of 2-months to 5-years. These checklists can be valuable tools when speaking with your child's pediatrician about concerns.

It is important to note that a checklist is not a substitute for an evaluation by a pediatrician or developmental specialist. You should always take your children to their regular well visits as recommended by their pediatrician.

When you have a solid understanding of your child's developmental needs and goals and use that information to support your child as they grow, you help your child build confidence and develop self-worth.

Reflective Questions

1. What are the behaviors your child has that most frustrate you the most?

_____

_____

_____

2. How did your parents react when you accomplished a new task?

_____

_____

_____

3. How did your parents react when you made a mistake or failed at a task?

_____

_____

_____

4. Why is it important for parents to have a general understanding of developmental milestones?

_____

_____

_____

5. Before reading this section, how much of an understanding did you have of developmental milestones?

_____

_____

Chapter One Quiz A

1. True or False: All children should be reaching developmental milestones at the same time.
2. True or False: If your child is late developing one milestone, it is a major red flag that something is wrong.
3. True or False: When you support your child and understand developmental milestones, you can help build your child's confidence.
4. At what age is it typical for a child to begin walking?
5. At what age is it typical for a child to use scissors with ease?
6. True or False: A child who is 3 years old should be able to read.
7. True or False: If you use a developmental checklist, your child does not need to see a pediatrician regularly.
8. True or False: Babies 6-9 months can point at things.
9. At what age should a child be able to climb up and down the stairs?
10. True or False: Children who are 7 years old tend to ask a lot of questions.

QUIZ A ANSWER GUIDE:

1: False. 2: False. 3: True. 4: 1 year – 18 months. 5: 5-6 years. 6: False. 7:False. 8: True. 9: 2 years. 10: True

Supporting Your Child's Development

Understanding your child's development is step one; supporting them as they develop is step two. Patience is critical when it comes to supporting your child's development. Think of a time in your past when you learned a new skill; it likely took time and patience with yourself to develop that skill; perhaps a boss or mentor was patient with you while you learned. The same goes for children; they need you to be patient as they grow and develop. What makes it even more challenging for a child to learn is that their mental acuity and physical dexterity are still developing.

Imagine how frustrating it must be to be learning so many new skills when your body and brain are still developing! One of the most incredible things a parent can do for a child is playing with them! Play is the essential way children learn. When parents make learning fun, children are more willing to participate. Getting down on your child's level and interacting with them also create a strong parent-child bond that supports secure attachment development.

A child who has developed a secure attachment with their parent or caregiver is more likely to explore and experiment in their environment, develop self-confidence, express less aggression, and demonstrate more empathy.

You can also support your child's development by speaking with them as they play and asking open-ended questions. Open-ended questions require children to think abstractly and encourage their language development. Examples of open-ended questions are, "Why did you use all the blue blocks?" or "What type of house do you think we should build for the tiger?" Open-ended questions start with why, how, what and require more than a one-word response. "What is your favorite color?" is not open-ended, "Why is green your favorite color?" is.

Open-ended questions can be used during play and while on walks outside, going through the grocery store, reading a book, or actively watching educational TV together. Passively watching TV together does not count as quality time with your child. However, if you turn it into an active situation by discussing what is happening and asking questions, it can benefit your child's development.

There have been recent studies done on active screen time versus passive screen time. Active screen time is still screen time and should not be overused, but active screen time requires your child to think, respond, and engage.

Additional ways to support your child's development are providing a loving and warm environment, providing their basic needs, setting up routines and schedules, and using appropriate discipline. As we go through this workbook, we will delve further into these concepts and provide in-depth strategies and information to support you in your parenting.

Reflective Questions

1. What are three things you can do you help support your child's development right now?

_____

_____

_____

_____

2. Choose one or two of your child's favorite books or TV shows and develop 10 open-ended questions you could ask.

_____

_____

_____

_____

3. Did you feel supported as a young child? Why or why not?

_____

_____

_____

_____

4. Why is it essential to support your child's development?

_____

_____

_____

_____

Children with Special Needs

Parenting a child is challenging enough on its own but parenting a child with special needs adds another layer of difficulties and challenges. Parenting a special needs child takes an emotional and physical toll on a parent and is often stressful. It is essential that you have a strong support system if you are the parent of a special needs child.

The term special needs is a broad term that refers to any individual that has been diagnosed with a developmental delay, chronic medical condition, mental health or neurodivergent condition, or congenital condition. Most children with special needs are able to live full and fulfilling lives when they receive adequate support and education.

Development Delay Categories and Definitions

✓ Physical Disabilities are conditions that affect the mobility, dexterity, capacity, or stamina of a child; it affects some aspect of their physical abilities.

✓ Neurodivergent Conditions are conditions that affect a person's intellectual and cognitive abilities.

✓ Developmental Delays are when a child is not developing at what is considered a typical rate. They may be late to walk or speak, or they may struggle with a learning disorder. Some children simply have a delay and will naturally or, with a bit of guidance, catch up. Others have severe developmental delays due to a broader disability and may require continued treatment and therapy.

✓ Chronic Medical Conditions are situations a child may not have been born with or developed no symptoms of until later. Many chronic conditions become life-long conditions that require continual care.

✓ Congenital Conditions are disabilities or diseases that a child was born with. Often with modern testing and ultrasounds, parents are aware of these conditions before birth. Congenital conditions are often a result of a chromosomal abnormality, but some, like fetal alcohol syndrome, are caused during pregnancy.

Physical Disabilities	Neurodivergent Conditions	Developmental Delays	Chronic Medical Conditions	Congenital Conditions
Use of a wheelchair	ADHD	Language/Speech	Cancer	Cerebral Palsy
Epilepsy	Dyslexia/Dyscalculia	Cognitive	Heart Conditions	Dwarfism
Vision loss/Blindness	Gifted/Talented	Physical, i.e., walking, low muscle tone	Asthma	Fetal Alcohol Syndrome
Hearing loss/Deafness	Depression/Anxiety		Food Allergies	Cleft Lip/Cleft Palate
	Asperger's/Autism			Down Syndrome

The chart above outlines some common disabilities children may face. Many of the above disabilities could fit in more than one category, and it is not uncommon for children who have one disability to have more than one. Some disabilities are short-term; for example, your child breaks their leg and needs to be in a wheelchair for six weeks. Most, however, are life-long conditions, and the sooner a child receives early intervention and educational support, the more successful they are likely to be.

Early Intervention

According to the CDC, Early Intervention is the term used to describe the services and supports available to babies and young children with developmental delays and disabilities and their families.

If your child qualifies for services, they are free of charge. It is the parent's responsibility to contact the appropriate agency in your state for your child to be evaluated. If you are unsure where to go, check your state's education website, talk to your child's childcare center, or ask your pediatrician.

You do not need a referral from a doctor to seek services. If you feel your child may have a disability or developmental delay, your child can be evaluated through your county or state's early intervention program. Early intervention services typically serve children 6-years of age and under. Once your child is school age, similar free services are available, but they would be evaluated through the state education department. Services for young children are typically broken down even further into birth-three and then three-six. Each state is different, so you will need to research what options are available for you and your child.

Most early intervention providers will perform services in your home or at your child's preschool or daycare center, making it easier on parents who work. The same will happen for school-age children who receive services; they will typically be included in your child's school day. You can, of course, always seek private services if your child does not qualify for free services and many insurance plans cover a limited number of sessions of services such as physical therapy, occupational therapy, and speech.

Early intervention is key to a child with a disability's success. No parent wants to hear that their child is "different," and some people fear having their child labeled. However, studies show that intervention provided early on is more effective than later in life . This is because the human brain goes through more development from birth through age five than at any other point in our growth.

Reflective Questions

1. What does it mean to have a disability or developmental delay?

_____

_____

_____

_____

2. Do you have any fears or concerns about having a child with a disability or developmental delay? Why or why not? (If you have a child with a disability or delay, describe your feelings).

_____

_____

_____

_____

3. What is your personal experience with individuals who have disabilities or developmental delays?

_____

_____

_____

_____

4. What is Early Intervention, and why is it so important?

_____

_____

_____

_____

5. Who is your support system as a parent? Why is it important to have a support system?

_____

_____

_____

_____

Child Abuse & Neglect

The information presented in this section may be upsetting for some, especially if you were the victim of abuse or neglect as a child. This section aims to outline the definitions and warning signs of abuse and neglect for educational purposes.

There are four categories of child abuse: Physical, Emotional, Sexual, and Neglect.

Definition of Child Abuse: Child abuse is when a parent or caregiver, whether through purposeful action or failing to act, causes injury, death, emotional harm, or risk of serious harm to a child.

Physical Abuse

Physical abuse is when an adult causes non-accidental injury to a child. The following are considered physical abuse: kicking, punching, whipping, bruises, blisters, cuts, burns, internal injuries, brain damage, broken bones, sprained muscles.

Physical actions that do not injure or impair a child, such as spanking, are not considered child abuse; however, physical discipline causes emotional and psychological damage. We will discuss spanking and alternative forms of discipline further in Chapter Five.

Physical Signs of Physical Abuse	Bruises, marks, burns, blisters, cuts, broken bones	Injuries in various stages of healing	Injuries on multiple parts of the body	Marks with a distinctive shape, for example, a cigarette burn or iron	Marks/Injuries seem to appear on a schedule, for example, after the weekend
Behavioral Signs of Physical Abuse	Withdrawn, depressed, fearful, or anxious	Aggression towards peers or animals	Extremely violent themes in their play, art, etc.	Nightmares and insomnia	Seems afraid of parents and other adults

Emotional Abuse

Emotional abuse is when a parent or caregiver harms a child's mental or social development or causes severe emotional harm.

Emotional abuse includes rejecting or ignoring a child, shaming, and humiliating a child, terrorizing a child, isolating a child, or forcing them to engage in corruptive behavior.

Physical Signs of Emotional Abuse	Developmental Delays	Bedwetting, frequent accidents after being potty trained	Speech disorders	Health problems	Frequent, noticeable weight fluctuation
Behavioral Signs of Emotional Abuse	Habits such as sucking, biting, or rocking	Extreme emotions, aggression, or withdrawal	Phobias, anxiety, sleep disorders	Destructive social behaviors: lying, stealing, cheating, violence	Suicidal thoughts or behaviors

Sexual Abuse

Sexual abuse is when an adult uses a child for sexual purposes or engages in sexual acts with a child. It also includes when older children use younger children for sexual gratification.

Sexual abuse includes non-contact abuse (exposure or use of child pornography), forcing a child to watch sexual acts, inappropriate sexual talk, contact abuse, fondling a child's genitals, penetration, making a child perform a sex act, exploitation, child prostitution.

Physical Signs of Sexual Abuse	Difficulty sitting or walking	Bowel problems. Frequent urinary tract infections.	Bleeding or bruising of the genital area.	Presence of a sexually transmitted disease or related symptoms.	Torn, stained, or bloody undergarments
Behavioral Signs of Sexual Abuse	Withdrawn, depressed, fearful, or anxious	Eating disorders. Preoccupation with body	Acting out sexually. Advanced sexual knowledge.	Nightmares and insomnia. Fear of bedtime.	Aggression, running away, suicidal thoughts.

Neglect

Physical Signs of Neglect	Clothing that doesn't fit or is dirty	Very low body weight for their age	Often tired, sleepy, or listless	Untreated medical conditions	Poor hygiene, body odor
Behavioral Signs of Neglect	Intentionally skipping school or not attending school	Talks about having to care for younger siblings	Stockpiles food or hoards food	Neglecting homework	Frequently misses obligations: school clubs

Neglect is when a parent or caregiver does not provide adequate care, nutrition, medical attention, supervision, education and does not support a child's wellbeing.

Types of neglect include emotional neglect, medical neglect, educational neglect, and physical neglect (lack of proper supervision).

Child abuse and neglect is commonly a cyclical pattern. Parents who were abused and neglected as children are left with emotional scars that can manifest in repeating the same behaviors that hurt them. But just because you were abused does not automatically mean you will abuse your children.

In fact less than half of people who were abused, roughly 30%, will also abuse their children.

If you were a victim of abuse or neglect, it is important to seek professional help to heal you and help your child.

If you suspect a child is being abused, you can report your suspicions anonymously. Proof is not needed to report suspected abuse.

If you fear you may be in danger of abusing your child or need help for a child already being abused, call The Childhelp National Child Abuse Hotline at 1-800-422-4453 or live chat on their website www.childhelp.org/hotline

You can also visit www.childwelfare.gov to find your local or state abuse reporting phone numbers.

> ## If you or a child are in immediate danger, call 9-1-1

Below Statistics on abuse courtesy of the American Society for the Positive Care of Children

- ✓ The highest rate of child abuse is in children under one (25.7 per 100 children)
- ✓ 14% of men and 36% of women in prison were abused as children
- ✓ In 2019 it was estimated 1,840 children died from child abuse
- ✓ Nearly 61,000 children are sexually abused
- ✓ Children who experience neglect and abuse are 9 times more likely to engage in criminal activity
- ✓ Boys are more like to die from abuse than girls (2.98% vs. 2.2%)
- ✓ 10.4% of sex trafficking cases involve boys

Reflective Questions

1. Were you abused or neglected as a child? How has that affected you as an adult? If you were not abused as a child, do you know someone who was?

_____

_____

_____

_____

2. Reflect on a time you were angry with your child; how did you handle that anger? Was it handled appropriately? Why or why not?

_____

_____

_____

_____

Chapter One Quiz B

1. Which of the following are the four types of abuse?
   a. Physical Abuse, Mental Abuse, Sexual Abuse & Emotional Neglect
   b. Physical Abuse, Emotional Abuse, Sexual Abuse, & Neglect
   c. Physical Abuse, Emotional Neglect, Sexual Abuse, & Medical Neglect
   d. Physical Abuse, Emotional Abuse, Sexual Abuse, & Medical Neglect

2. True or False: Physically punishing your child in any form is ok if it doesn't leave a lasting mark.
3. True or False: Bedwetting and accidents after a child has been potty-trained is a possible sign of abuse.
4. Which of the following set of symptoms are signs of sexual abuse?
   a. Stained undergarments, fear, and anxiety, insomnia
   b. Difficulty walking or sitting, missing school, advanced sexual knowledge
   c. Depression, eating disorders, frequent urinary tract infections
   d. All of the Above

5. True or False: Educational Neglect is a form of abuse
6. True or False: When reporting suspected abuse, you must provide your name and phone number
7. True or False: If you were abused as a child, you have a 50% chance of abusing your children.
8. True or False: Boys can be victims of sexual abuse and sex trafficking.
9. Which of the following are considered neglect? Select all that apply.
   a. Lack of proper medical treatment.
   b. Not providing your child with their favorite food every day.
   c. Failing to provide proper supervision for your child.
   d. Grounding them and not letting them play video games for a week.

10. True or False: If you were the victim of abuse or neglect, you should seek mental health treatment.

QUIZ B ANSWER GUIDE

1: B. 2: False. 3: True. 4: D. 5: True. 6: False. 7: False. 8: True 9: A and C. 10: True

Chapter Two
Communication

The Importance of Communication

This workbook is likely not the first time you have heard how essential communication skills are to relationships. Communication is an essential part of the human experience. Humans are social beings and therefore require interactions with others to thrive. Numerous studies completed show that infants who do not receive adequate physical touch and interaction with adults often fail to thrive, are at a higher risk of social and emotional problems and may even die.

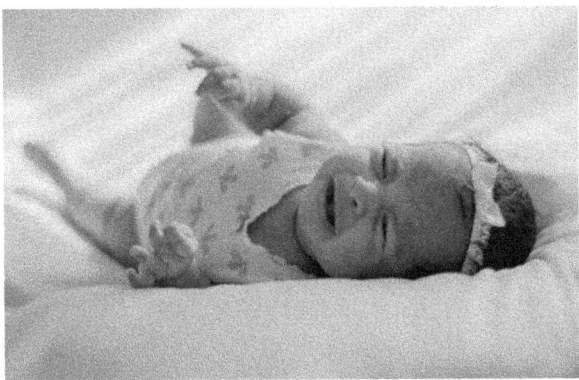

Communication between a parent and their child is vital to a child's language development, social development, and the bond between parent and child. It is also crucial that parents know how to effectively communicate with the other adults in their child's life, including medical professionals, caregivers, teachers, family members, and co-parents.

This chapter of the workbook will walk you through productive, effective ad meaningful ways not only to communicate with your child but to communicate with the other important people in your child's life.

Talking with Children

Notice the heading of this section is talking with children, not to children. To effectively communicate with your child, you need to make them a part of the conversation. Even young children can be active participants in conversations when they are taught their words have value and are worth listening to.

There is always a reason behind every behavior and action a child makes, even if it does not seem linear or clear cut to us as adults. When you slow down and engage your child in conversation, you will better understand their motivation. You can then use that understanding to teach them. Is hitting their brother wrong? Absolutely! But when you understand that your child hit their brother because their brother had been teasing them for the last ten minutes, you can work with your child on more appropriate ways to handle their anger and frustration.

When adults yell, children are frightened, and they stop listening and processing what is being said. Imagine a time your boss or a friend yelled at you or was disappointed with you. You probably began to feel flushed and upset as cortisol flooded your system; you probably were already coming up with a counterargument in your head and, therefore, not really listening to what they were saying.

Now imagine if your boss was three or four times the size of you. That's scary, and it's not an effective way to communicate with anyone, let alone a child.

To effectively communicate in any situation, we must first calm ourselves. If your child has behaved in a way that makes you feel like your blood is boiling, take a step back and calm down. It is ok to say to your child, "I am feeling extremely angry right now, but I need to take a time out before I can talk to you." Yes, adults can use time-outs! In its essence a time out is an opportunity for the adult or child to calm down, not a punishment.

Take yourself to a quiet room and breathe deeply. Then, when you are ready, sit down and calmly talk with your child.

Speaking calmly to children is much more effective than yelling. This is especially the case with older children and teenagers. Plus, when we as adults yell, we are basically having a temper tantrum and show our kids that that type of behavior is acceptable. Additionally, children of all ages feel frightened when they believe their parents have no control. When we slow down and speak calmly and quietly, it forces our children to tune in and listen.

When speaking to your child get down on their child's level when speaking to them. When you loom over your child, yes, you have the position of authority, but if the goal is effective communication, getting onto their level makes them feel safer and communicates you are willing to hear what they have to say.

Especially when your child is receiving a consequence, getting on their level is a way to treat them respectfully and to have them listen more efficiently. If we want our children to show respect, we must lead by example. Fear is never an effective method of discipline or communication. We will cover this more in-depth in Chapter Five.

Even the youngest children have something to say! Find time each day to engage in conversation with your child. You can talk to a baby and allow them space to babble back, you can talk to a toddler about their drawing or favorite toy. Your preschooler likely has a thousand questions about everything, and your elementary schooler may need to talk about a fight with a friend. Even your teenager who acts like they do not want to talk to you still wants positive attention from you.

When your child is upset, embarrassed, sad, or angry they may not always want to talk in the moment. Let them know you are always available if and when they do want to talk. Do not force communication. If you have said your part or are trying to get your child to open up, simply let them know they can come to you. "I have to go fold the laundry, so I'll be in the bedroom if you need me." If you open up the lines of communication when your children are young and make them feel valued, they will learn it is always safe to talk to you when things are difficult which can be extremely beneficial as they approach adolescence.

Activities to Try

1. Take a Time Out. If your emotions are intense, put yourself in time out. You can lock yourself in the bathroom and put on some earbuds or go into your bedroom.
   - Communicate with your child that you need to talk with them about the situation but that you need some time to calm down and think.
2. Consider implementing family meetings on a weekly or twice-monthly basis. This method works well with older children and teens. Family meetings provide a safe space to discuss topics of concern or to put in place new guidelines.
3. Ban cellphones and electronics at the breakfast or dinner table. It can be difficult for families to communicate because everyone has a device.
   - Choose a meal that you typically enjoy with your children; put phones away, yours too- lead by example!
4. Here are some questions to ask your child to encourage communication. The items in parenthesis are examples and can be changed based on the situation.

- What were you feeling when you (threw that toy)?
- Can you explain your thought process to me?
- I don't understand (why you like this music). Can you explain why it is important to you?
- Tell me your favorite and least favorite thing about your day.
- What was something that happened today that made you smile?
- How did (choir practice) go today?
- Can you teach me one thing you learned today?

Reflective Questions

1. Think of a time when your communication with your child was ineffective. Knowing what you know now, what made it ineffective? What could you do differently?

_____

_____

_____

2. What are some things that make it difficult for you to talk to your child effectively?

_____

_____

_____

_____

3. What was the communication style like between you and your parents? What worked well and what as a child or teen do you think would have helped you communicate better with your parents?

_____

_____

_____

_____

Chapter Two Quiz A

1. True or False: Children respond best to yelling.
2. True or False: Getting down onto your child's level can help them feel safe.
3. Which of the following questions is NOT an effective way to start a conversation with your child?
   a. Tell me about your soccer practice?
   b. What's wrong with you? Why would you do that?
   c. I don't understand why you want to learn Chinese. Can you explain it to me?
   d. Where did you and your friends go after school today?
4. Which of the following statements are true? Select all the are correct.
   a. Fear is an effective way to discipline children
   b. Speaking calmly and quietly forces children to pay attention.
   c. There is no point in talking to babies since they cannot speak yet.
   d. It helps communication if your child knows you are always available to them when needed.
5. True or False: When children feel their opinion is valued, they are more likely to talk and listen.

QUIZ B ANSWER GUIDE

1: False. 2: True. 3: B. 4: B & D. 5: True

Communicating with Caregivers & Teachers

If you're like many modern parents, your children will spend some time in a child care center or be cared for by a nanny or home provider. Even if you stay home with your child until kindergarten, you will likely have the occasional babysitter and eventually they will be in the care of a teacher. Possessing the tools to communicate with these individuals effectively is essential to your child's success.

The first part of effective communication with caregivers and teachers is understanding that they are often experts on the age group they work with. Quality childcare providers and teachers understand child development and what behaviors are typical and not typical. If a teacher or caregiver comes to you with concerns, be a receptive listener. In the end, you may not agree with their assessment, but being friendly and open to communication, even about the negative aspects, builds a stronger relationship.

No teacher wants to come to a parent with concerns, so understand that when they reach out to you, they have probably observed and recorded documentation on your child for weeks or months before approaching you.

Teachers are likely just as nervous as you are when a phone call or meeting takes place! You know your child best, but even if you disagree with a caregiver or teacher's assessment, seek a second opinion instead of just disregarding it.

Parents need to be open and honest with caregivers and teachers about their child's life, particularly any changes. As a parent, you may not realize that grandma moving in or the family cat dying makes a big difference, but these changes can be life-altering to children. Even fun events can cause behavior changes. Consider a child right before their birthday or a major holiday; their behavior usually intensifies. Changes, even small ones, can affect your child. Informing your child's caregiver of any changes to their routine or life helps the teacher better prepare.

Children can sense the tension between adults, so if you disagree with their teacher's opinion, it is important to present a united front. The more open the communication chain between parent and caregiver or teacher, the better they can work as a team for the child. If the situation feels tense request a meeting with a third party present such as a school administrator or guidance counselor.

Situations that might affect your child:

- Moving
- Having a new sibling/pregnancy
- Relative moving in or out of the home
- Changing schools
- Switching bedrooms/switching from a crib to bed
- Divorce
- Death of family or pet
- Getting a new pet
- Change in routine/Different parent picking up or dropping off
- A parent losing or switching jobs
- Vacation or holiday
- Upcoming sports games, performance, school projects, etc.
- A parent away on travel or a parent deployed in the military
- A change in babysitters or afterschool program

Reflective Questions

1. Do you consider communication with teachers and caregivers important? Why or why not?

_____

_____

_____

_____

2. What are some changes or events coming up in your child's life that may be affecting them?

_____

_____

_____

_____

Communicating with Family

Everyone has an opinion on how to raise your child, especially family members. Picture the phrase, "It takes a village." This expression exists because, in early human society, the community or village did help raise each child. Women had aunts, sisters, mothers, and female village elders to teach them everything they needed to know about pregnancy, giving birth, breastfeeding, and raising their children. Now, for better or worse, we have the internet which often overloads parents with too much information; it seems like everyone is telling you that you are doing it wrong.

Today's parents often struggle to raise their kids, often far away from a strong supportive unit and while holding down a job or two.

Nonetheless, whether your mother-in-law lives with you or she lives 2,000 miles away, communication with family is an essential part of maintaining a healthy relationship for both you and your child.

If a family member is taking care of your child regularly or as full-time childcare, they must understand the values you wish to teach your child. If your aunt strongly believes in attending church every Sunday and you plan to raise your child secularly, this is a conversation you must have beforehand. Similarly, if you do not believe in spanking, but your mother watching your child does, guidelines need to be established.

Family members can be an invaluable source of wisdom, but generational and sometimes cultural differences can cause tensions. Any conversations about expectations, the child's behavior, discipline, and especially tense subjects should be discussed privately away from the child. Children need to feel secure, and one of the ways to provide security is when all the adults in their life present as a united front.

It can feel challenging to approach sensitive topics with a family member. One option is to prime the other person by saying something like, "Before you watch Sammie, there are a few things I want to discuss with you; when is a good time?" Another option is to take the conversation to a public place such as the park or a coffee shop. People tend to control their emotions better when others are watching. Be prepared to explain why specific issues are important; it might help if you have statistics or facts to back you up.

Consider preparing talking points on index cards; if you are nervous, you may forget what you want to say. Avoid phone calls and text is possible. Face-to-face communication is always best as intonation and voice timbre cannot be sent via email or text and facial expressions cannot be seen over the phone.

If something occurred that prompted the need for a talk, take the time to cool down before responding. When we rush to respond in anger or frustration, we often regret the results.

Ultimately, the important thing is your child, and you may need to pick your battles. If your sister agrees to watch your child two days a week so you can work, is it worth fighting over whether the chicken nuggets are organic? Decide which items in your child-rearing are non-negotiable, then work on letting the others go if you and your family member cannot see eye to eye.

Reflective Questions

1. Does discussing challenging situations with your family make you uncomfortable? Why or why not?

_____

_____

_____

_____

2. What are some things you can do to prepare for a difficult conversation?

_____

_____

_____

_____

3. What topics might come up with a family member about your child or your parenting style?

_____

_____

_____

_____

4. When it comes to a family member watching your child, what are your non-negotiables?

_____

_____

_____

_____

Communicating with Doctors and Health Professionals

The final group of people you will have regular interactions with are your child's pediatrician, dentist, eye doctor, and other health professionals they may need to visit. A baby and young child need to see a pediatrician regularly. After your baby is born, it may feel like you live at the doctor's!

The recommended schedule for a baby's check-up and immunization schedule is as follows:

- days post-birth
- 1 month
- 2 months
- 4 months
- 6 months
- 9 months
- 12 months
- 15 months

- 18 months
- 24 months

It is essential for your baby's health to make and keep these appointments even if everything seems to be "ok."

It is a good idea to write down any questions or concerns you have for the doctor in a notebook as they arise. It can be easy to forget details when you are sitting in the office with the doctor. This is especially important if you have concerns about your child's development or have noticed any unusual symptoms.

Your pediatrician will likely have you fill out an Ages and Stages questionnaire or similar document at each visit. Answering these questions truthfully will give your pediatrician the most accurate information and better prepare them to treat your child.

Do not feel embarrassed if your child is not meeting specific milestones or if you are having difficulty meeting their nutritional needs. The pediatrician can help you by providing you with additional resources such as information on:

- Supplemental Nutrition Program (SNAP)
- Special Supplemental Nutrition Program for Women, Infants, and Children (WIC)
- Specialists to address any developmental concerns; remember all children develop at their own pace.

It is essential to remember that the doctors, nurses, and other health professionals your child visits are there to help you. Being open and honest about your child's development, home life, and other health-related issues is the best way to help your child grow up healthy.

Dentists & Optometrists

It is recommended by the American Dental Association (ADA) that your child see a dentist at six months or when their first tooth erupts. Dental decay affects 1 out of every child under the age of 5. When choosing a dentist, it is recommended to look specifically for a pediatric dentist since they will be better equipped to work with wiggly and fearful children.

The American Optometric Society recommends a child receiving a screening by an optometrist before 24 months of age, then again, for a comprehensive screening between the ages of 3 and 5. One in four children suffers from an eyesight problem that affects their education and learning. Vision screenings by a school or pediatrician are a good starting point, but they do not replace a comprehensive screening by an eye doctor.

We will cover additional information about health and safety, dentists, eye doctors, and other health specialists in-depth in Chapter Four.

Chapter Two Quiz B

1. True or False: If your child seems to be developing, typically, it is ok to skip well visits.
2. True or False: Writing down concerns and questions for the doctor ahead of time can help you remember important information.
3. What are the two supplemental food programs you can apply for if you need help providing nutritious food for your child?
   a. SNAP & WIC
   b. SNAP & WCC

    c. NSAP & WIC

    d. NSAP & WCC

1. What is the name of the developmental questionnaire your pediatrician may ask you to fill out at well visits?

    a. Stages and Progressions

    b. Developmental Stages

    c. Ages and Development

    d. Ages & Stages

2. At what age should your child receive their first comprehensive eye exam

    e. Between 2-4

    f. Between 4-6

    g. Between 3-5

    h. Between 1-3

3. True or False: It is not important to tell your pediatrician everything because they will be able to look at your child and figure out any issues.

4. At what age should your child first see a dentist?

    i. 1 Year

    j. 6 Months

    k. 8 Months

    l. 2 Years

5. True or False: You should NOT feel embarrassed if your child is missing milestones, all children develop differently, and pediatricians can help guide you.

QUIZ B ANSWER GUIDE

1: False. 2: True. 3: A. 4: D. 5: C. 6: False. 7: B. 8: True

Chapter Three
Safety

Basic Child Safety

One of your primary jobs as a parent is to keep your child safe and free from harm. Of course, accidents happen, and when they do, we are there to comfort our children and fix the boo-boos. However, many childhood accidents, both big and small, can be prevented with a basic understanding of child safety.

Childproofing your home is your first line of defense. Cabinets within your child's reach should have childproof locks, baby gates should be secured near stairs, windows and doors should have locks and pinch guards, heavy furniture should be secured to the wall, cords should be out of reach, and outlets should have safety covers.

When childproofing your home, get down on your child's level and look around you. What potential hazards or temptations do you see? Children love to explore, so even the most benign things to you may be tempting to them.

According to the CDC, unintentional accidents are the number one cause of death of children in the United States each year. Many of these accidents are caused by accidental drowning, poisoning, traffic accidents, and falls.

As your children grow, talk to them about various dangers. Discuss looking both ways before crossing the street and that they should never swim without an adult present. You should address stranger danger, wearing a seatbelt, and staying in their car seat while the vehicle is in motion. As you approach the teen years, you should address the dangers of drugs and alcohol and discuss safe sex, consent, and what to do if they find themselves in a dangerous situation.

Home and Safety Check List

Fall Prevention	Clear clutter from floors	Never leave babies unattended on raise surfaces	Wipe up spills. Keep the floor dry.	Keep windows and doors locked.	Ensure baby gates are secure.	Use safety harnesses in highchairs.	Lower the crib mattress once the baby can sit up.
Choking Prevention	Use age-appropriate toys.	Keep small objects out of reach.	Cut their food into bite-size pieces.	Balloons, strings, and plastic bags should be kept out of reach.	Children under 18 months should not use a pillow.	Do not leave a baby unattended while eating or drinking.	Keep dry pet food out of reach.
Burn Prevention	Never drink hot liquids while holding your baby.	Keep your child out of the kitchen when cooking.	Check the bath water temperature before placing the baby in the tub.	Do not microwave baby food or bottles as heating is uneven.	Keep all hot objects out of your child's reach: irons, curling irons	Do not use candles around your child.	Cover wall sockets.
Poisoning Prevention	Keep cabinets with cleaners and solutions locked.	Keep medicines out of reach.	DO NOT tell children medicine is candy or sweets.	Ensure toys and eating utensils, plates, cups are non-toxic.	Do not keep poisonous plants in the home.		

Reflective Questions

1. After reading this introduction, what potential dangers does your home currently pose to your child?

_____

_____

_____

_____

2. What steps can you take to childproof your home?

_____

_____

_____

_____

CPR/First Aid

Disclaimer: This Guide Is In No Way A Substitute For Medical Attention. The Information Presented Here Is Only A Guideline To Basic First Aid.

CPR stands for cardiopulmonary resuscitation. It is an emergency lifesaving procedure performed when a person's heart stops beating. Anyone can become certified in CPR, and it is recommended that all new parents do so. Classes can be found in a variety of places, such as libraries, hospitals, and community centers.

Typically, when CPR certification is being offered, dual certification in First Aid is also available simultaneously. These classes can take anywhere from 4-8 hours but are well worth the time and effort. Even if you cannot earn official certification in CPR and First Aid, the American Heart Association's website offers guides and materials that can help teach you the basics.

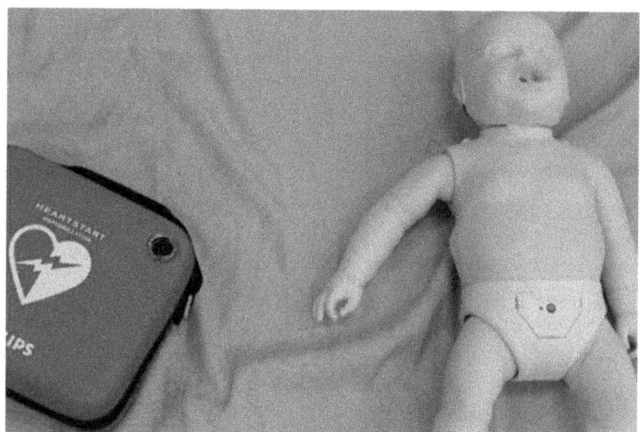

Guidelines have changed over the years on how to administer CPR to adults and children. For the most up-to-date information, visit www.redcross.org or the American Heart Association. However, if your child is unresponsive or unconscious, think ABC. Airway. Breathing. Circulation.

To perform chest compressions, push down hard and fast in the middle of their chest. For a baby, use two fingers, a child one hand, a teen or adult two hands.

ALWAYS CALL 9-1-1 if you find your child or anyone else unresponsive and not breathing.

First Aid

Cuts and Scrapes: Clean the wound with soap and water. Apply a clean bandage. If the wound is bleeding, apply direct pressure with a clean cloth and, if possible, raise the wound above the heart.

Burns: Rinse the burn in cool water (not cold) for several minutes, apply a clean, soft non-stick bandage. Do not break open any blisters that form.

Choking: If a person is coughing or talking, they are not choking. If they cannot talk or make noise, are gasping or wheezing, begin to turn blue, or appear panicked, they are likely choking.

To perform the Heimlich maneuver:

1. Stand behind the person and lean them slightly forward
2. Put your arms around their waist
3. Clench a fist and place it between their navel and rib cage
4. Grab your fist with your other hand
5. Pull the clenched fist sharply backward and upward under their rib cage in 5 quick thrusts. Repeat until the object is coughed up.

Broken Bones, Fractures & Sprains: All broken bones and fractures should be treated by a medical professional. If the child is unconscious and there is a suspected spinal injury, DO NOT move them.

However, if the child is conscious and there is NOT a suspected injury to the spine, head, hip, or pelvis, you can take the following steps until you can seek care.

- Use a splint or padding to keep the injury still
- Wrap an ice pack in a towel or t-shirt and place on injury
- For limbs, elevate them
- Provide pain medication such as ibuprofen, acetaminophen or naproxen. Be sure to administer the proper dosage for your child's age and weight.

Nosebleeds: Lean the head slightly forward. Pinch the nose below the bridge but without closing the nostrils. Apply a cold pack to the nose.

If your child has frequent nosebleeds or nosebleeds that will not stop after 15 minutes, consult their pediatrician.

Bee Stings & Insect Bites: Bee stings, in particular, can cause a severe allergic reaction in some people, and these allergies can develop at any time. If your child is stung by a bee, look for signs of an allergic reaction, including swelling away from the area that was stung, hives, itching, impaired breathing, chest pain, confusions, and dizziness.

If you notice ANY of these signs, call 9-1-1.

General first aid for stings and insect bites: Get the stinger out as quickly as possible, wash the bite with soap and water, and use a cold pack to reduce swelling. You can also administer an antihistamine to help with swelling.

Choking & Strangulation Hazards

One way young children learn is by putting everything in their mouths, and we mean EVERYTHING. A young child is hard-wired to use their 5-senses to explore the world around them. Therefore, it is a parent's job to reduce the risk of choking by keeping potential hazards away from their child.

A general rule to follow is, if it can fit in their mouth or is smaller than their fist, keep it out of reach.

All cords, wires, string, rope, ribbon, etc., should be kept out of your baby's reach to prevent strangulation. Mobiles hung above your baby's crib should be removed once they can sit up and only used under adult supervision.

If your baby goes to bed with a pacifier, be sure to remove pacifier clips or ribbons before placing them in the crib.

Toy manufacturers are required to label toys under a specific size as a potential choking hazard, so be sure to purchase age-appropriate toys for your child. Even so, many three and four-year-old children still moth objects, so be aware of your child's tendencies and keep small objects away if this is the case for you.

Food

Many foods pose a choking risk to small children. Popcorn should NEVER be served to children under the age of three. Opt for an alternative such as Pirate Booty or puffed rice cakes. Food should always be cut lengthwise and then quartered for younger children, not in a circular shape. Circular cut food can quickly become lodges in a child's throat.

Foods to Avoid for Children Under 3

Hot Dogs	Dried Fruit	Grapes	Pretzels	Raw Veggies
Nuts	Cubed Cheese	Tortilla Chips	Hard Candy & Gum	Bread

Other choking hazards around the home are buttons, marbles, paperclips, magnets, small knobs, coins, medications, batteries, laundry pods, older sibling's toys, pet food, food dropped on the floor, plastic bags, and balloons.

Remember, it should be considered a choking hazard if it is smaller than your baby's first.

Chapter Three Quiz A

1. Of the following lists, which one contains choking hazards for young children:
   a. Pirate Booty, cooked peas, quartered grapes, diced chicken
   b. Popcorn, whole grapes, hot dogs, cubed cheese
   c. Cooked peas, quartered grapes, puffed rice, Cheerios
   d. Pirate Booty, puffed rice, Cheerios, quartered grapes

2. True or False: A pacifier clip is safe in your baby's crib as long as it is short.
3. True or False: Anything smaller than your baby's fist should be considered a choking hazard.
4. True or False: A child putting objects in their mouth is inappropriate and should be stopped.
5. Which of the following lists contains household choking and strangulation hazards for your child?
   a. Coins, pet food, balloons, & an older sibling's toys
   b. Marbles, cords, batteries, & wires
   c. Medications, batteries, laundry pods, & plastic bags
   d. All of the Above

QUIZ A ANSWER GUIDE

1: B. 2: False. 3: True. 4: False 5: D

Accidental Poisoning

Nearly half of all accidental poisoning calls made each year are for children under the age of six, and each year, roughly 38 children will die from ingesting poison. Many of these accidents could have been prevented with proper childproofing, storage, and supervision.

> If you suspect your child has ingested poison, call Poison Control at 1-800-222-1222 or Text the word POISON to 484848.

To prevent your child from accidental poisoning, it is crucial to lock up all cleaning supplies, bug sprays, detergents, medications, cosmetics, and personal care products. You can place childproof locks on all cabinets and closest containing these products, or better yet, store them out of reach of your child.

The top two dangers for accidental poisoning in a home are cosmetics/personal care products and cleaning supplies. A child proof-lid or cap does not guarantee that your child cannot open it. Proper storage is essential.

Another risk for accidental poisoning around the home is plants. There are many plants both inside and outside the home that pose a danger to your child. Some of the most common are:

- Philodendron, English Ivy, Easter Lily, Oleander, Daffodils, Mistletoe, Holly, Dieffenbachia, Peace Lily, Azalea, Morning Glory, and Fox Glove.

SIDS & Shaken Baby

Shaken Baby Syndrome is the leading cause of child abuse deaths in the United States. It is most common in infants under 6-months of age. 80% of children who survive suffer Shaken Baby Syndrome will have lifelong disabilities, and 25% of children who experience it die.

Shaken Baby Syndrome is the result of severe brain injury caused by a child being shaken. It is caused by the forceful shaking of the baby, usually when a caregiver is stressed and or angry.

If you feel stress because your baby won't stop crying, you should seek help from friends or family members. If needed, place the baby safely in their crib and walk away for 10-15 minutes while you calm yourself down. It is OK to let your baby cry; be sure to check on them regularly.

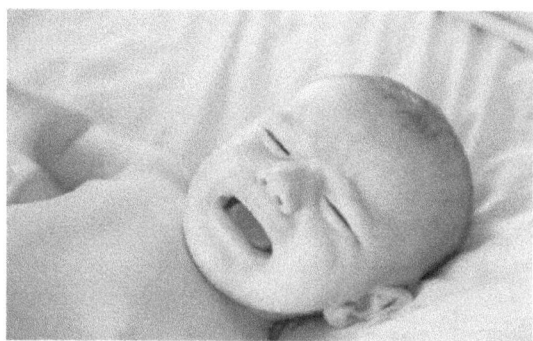

Exercise is important when facing stress. Take the baby for a walk or engage in exercise while they are playing or napping.

Use deep breathing exercises to help calm you do, participate in medication, yoga, or gentle stretching.

Soothing Your Baby

When your baby is crying, it may feel like nothing is going to help. That can make you as a parent feel helpless. Sometimes no matter what we try, babies will cry. It is their only form of communication, and unfortunately, we don't always know what a cry means.

There are some tricks you can try, however, that may help calm your child.

- Check the basics first. Are they hungry? Wet? Sleepy? Hot? Cold?
- Wrap or swaddled the baby snuggly in a blanket
- Rub your baby's back as you rock them
- Take your baby for a walk outside, or if you are stuck inside, walk them around the house in the stroller or a baby carrier
- Sing to them quietly, even if it is not an actual song
- Change environments. Your baby may be overstimulated (too much input) or under-stimulated (not enough input).
  - Switch rooms
  - Turn off the TV or music
  - Turn off the lights
  - Play music if it is quiet
  - Give them a new toy to play with

- Hold your baby and gently dance around to music.
- Wear earbuds or headphones to reduce the sound of crying
- Remember not to take crying personal

SIDS

SIDS is Sudden Infant Death Syndrome. It is the sudden and unexplained death of an infant under 12 months old. Its actual cause is unknown, and cases have drastically reduced in the last few decades, but there are still things that you can do to prevent the risk of SIDS.

Babies whose mothers smoke and drink alcohol while pregnant are at a higher risk of SIDS. Boys are also more common to die from SIDS than girls. Babies who live in a house with smokers are also at an increased risk.

Things you can do to reduce the risk of SIDS include:

- Using a firm crib mattress
- Allowing baby to sleep in the same room but NOT the same bed as you
- Breastfeeding
- Using a pacifier
- Keeping their room at a cool temperature – approximately 68 degrees
- DO NOT use crib bumpers, pillows, sheets, blankets, sleep positioners, stuffed animals, or anything else in the crib besides a snug-fitting crib sheet
- Place babies on their BACK to sleep
- DO not feed your baby honey
- Follow the recommended immunization schedule
- Use swaddles or footed pajamas if you are worried your baby will be cold

SIDS Prevention Check List

- ✓ Keep your crib away from windows or cords.
- ✓ Remove any stuffed animals, blankets, and toys from the crib.
- ✓ Do NOT use crib bumpers.
- ✓ Use a fitted sheet.
- ✓ Use a firm crib mattress.

- ✓ Keep the room temperature comfortable, 68-70 degrees Fahrenheit.
- ✓ Lay your baby to sleep on their back. Be sure to inform family and friends who care for your baby to do this as well.
- ✓ Give your baby a pacifier for sleeping. Remove any clips or cords before placing them in the crib.
- ✓ Do NOT smoke or allow anyone to smoke around your baby.
- ✓ Use a sleep sack or fitted pajamas to keep your baby comfortable.
- ✓ Breastfeed if possible.
- ✓ Sleep in the same room as your baby, but NOT the same bed.
- ✓ Use a baby monitor.

Tips to Reduce Stress

- ✓ Call a close friend or family member
- ✓ Go for a walk or jog
- ✓ Go out for coffee, lunch, or a drink with a friend
- ✓ Journal or use adult coloring books
- ✓ Practice Yoga or meditation
- ✓ Read
- ✓ Watch a favorite TV show or movie
- ✓ Dance around
- ✓ Bake or Cook something
- ✓ Take a bath or shower
- ✓ Light some candles or use an oil diffuser
- ✓ Take a nap
- ✓ Do a facial or foot soak
- ✓ Listen to music

Chapter Three Quiz B

1. True or False: Lying a baby on its back is best when sleeping.
2. True or False: The ideal room temperature for a baby to sleep in is warm, above 72 degrees.
3. Which of the following causes Shaken Baby Syndrome?
   a. A baby being left to cry it out in their crib.
   b. A caregiver yelling at a baby to stop crying.
   c. A caregiver forcefully shaking a baby.
   d. A caregiver aggressively pushing a stroller back and forth with the baby inside.
4. True or False: It is ok to use crib bumpers as long as you use a baby monitor.
5. The risk of SIDS can be reduced by which of the following?
   a. Keeping cigarette smoke away from your baby.
   b. Using a pacifier for sleeping.
   c. Using a sleep sack in place of a blanket.
   d. Using a firm crib mattress.
   e. All of the Above

6. SIDS stands for:
   a. Simple Infant Debilitating Syndrome
   b. Shaken Infant Death Syndrome
   c. Shaken Infant Debilitating Syndrome
   d. Sudden Infant Death Syndrome
7. True or False: Shaken Baby Syndrome is the number one cause of death by child abuse in the United States.
8. True or False: If your baby won't stop crying and you are feeling stressed, it is ok to lie them in their crib and walk away for 10-15 minutes.
9. True or False: SIDS is 100% avoidable
10. True or False: Shaken Baby Syndrome is 100% avoidable

QUIZ B ANSWER GUIDE

1: True. 2: False. 3: C. 4: False. 5: E. 6: D. 7: True. 8: True. 9: False. 10: True.

Car Seats

Injuries sustained due to a car crash are the number one cause of death in children aged 3-14 in the United States. A whopping 128,000 children, on average, are injured in car crashes each year. Many of these deaths and related injuries could have been prevented by the proper use of child restraints.

Statistics show that anywhere from 72% to 84% of child restraints are being misused in one way or another. The most common errors are children being in the wrong seat and the seat not being securely attached enough in the vehicle.

At the same time, these same studies show that 96% of these parents believe they are using their car seats correctly!

Car Seat Safety Tips

Place the car seat in the correct spot.	Avoid using a used car seat. If you do check the expiration date.	Read the manual to install the seat correctly.	Harness straps & chest clip should fit snugly at baby's chest – NOT stomach	Keep the seat REAR FACING as long as possible. Read manufacturer's recommendations.
Install car seats in the back seat.	Remove heavy coats and outerwear before buckling them in. Place a blanket over after buckling them in.	Use a booster seat with the shoulder and lap belt.	Keep using a booster seat until their feet can touch the ground (approx. 4' 9")	Use all the latches recommended by the manufacturer.

The DMV.org, National Highway Traffic Safety Administration NHTSA, and GEICO.com all have videos and how-to guides on correctly installing a car seat.

Parents should set a good example by always wearing their seatbelts and explaining to children the importance of a seat belt and how it works. Parents should refrain from participating in distracted driving, such as texting or talking on their phones while driving.

Internet Safety

A new danger modern parents must deal with is the internet. Children younger and younger have access to phones, tablets, and computers, and often we leave our children unsupervised with these devices. The recent COVID-19 pandemic made it so that virtually every child needed access to the internet for schooling and spent even more time online.

The internet is a fantastic invention and can be a handy tool, but many hidden dangers exist. Chief among these dangers is pornography or other inappropriate sexual content, severe violence, inappropriate language, sexual predators, and cyber-bullying.

Children are curious by nature and will want to explore the internet as much as anything else they have access to, so it is a parent's job to control what their child has access to. You will need to decide for your child what you consider appropriate and inappropriate based on their age and maturity level.

Tips to Keep Kids Safe

- Keep the use of computers and other electronic devices to public areas such as the living room, kitchen, or family room
- If your child is using electronics in their room, have them keep the door open.
- Use parental controls and set up family accounts so you can monitor the content they see and the sites they visit.
- Browse the computer history from time to time to watch for any potential red flags.
- Talk to your children about internet safety.
  - Never give your name, age, address, email, or phone number to a stranger
  - Never share a picture of yourself with a stranger
  - If someone is saying hurtful things or things that make you uncomfortable, speak to a trusted adult.
  - Do not accept friend requests from people you do not know personally
  - Never agree to meet anyone anywhere without a parent's permission and an adult with you.
- Create user profiles on social media sites your child likes so you can monitor their content.
- Revoke internet and electronic privileges if rules about internet safety are broken.
- Do not allow your child to have purchasing capabilities – remove all links to your bank accounts and credit card.
- Make sure your child knows you are a safe spot to come to no matter what!

Cyberbullying

Cyberbullying is a dangerous threat to your child's mental health and well-being. It can happen over social medial, gaming sites, email, text, messaging apps, online forums, and instant messaging. A 2019 study revealed that over 15% of high school students admitted to being cyberbullied. Cyberbullying can affect young children as well as a leading cause that contributes to teen suicide.

Many teens may be afraid to report their bullies, so be sure to offer a safe place for your child if they need to talk.

Familiarize yourself with the signs that your child may be being bullied:

- Slipping in grades, missed work
- Avoidance of favorite activities or clubs

- Weight loss, poor appetite or binge eating
- Frequently "losing" their items at school
- Difficulty sleeping, nightmares
- Skipping school or classes
- Becoming withdrawn or depressed
- Frequent or repeated self-hate speech, "I'm ugly," I'm so dumb"

Reflective Questions

1. Do you know what sites your child is typically on?

_____

_____

_____

2. Do you have parental controls set up on any sites?

_____

_____

_____

3. How often do you sit with your child and watch content together?

_____

_____

_____

4. What devices does your child have access to? Are they allowed to use them behind closed doors? How do you currently monitor what they see?

_____

_____

_____

5. Have you had a conversation with your child about internet safety? If not, write some prompts or a script for the conversation below.

_____

_____

_____

Chapter Four
Health & Hygiene

Regular Checkups

Taking your baby to the doctor regularly when they are first born is a must. In fact, in their first two years of life, they will see the doctor at least ten times, and that is not counting any sick visits should they need them! Establishing a good relationship with your pediatrician is essential to your child's overall health.

Regular checkups let you know if there are any health or development concerns you need to be aware of, and they let you know if your baby is developing at a typical rate. Most importantly, regular checkups are when your baby receives recommended immunizations that keep them healthy.

The recommended schedule for doctor visits and vaccinations is below:

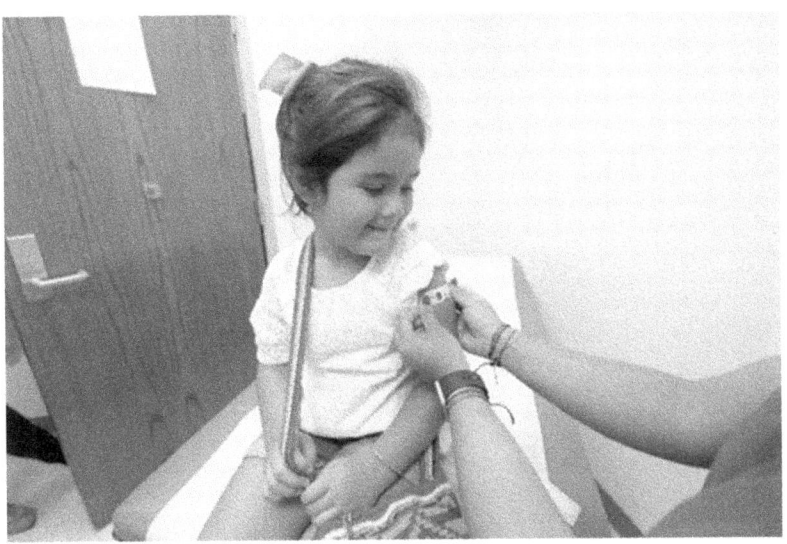

- days post-birth
- 1 month
- 2 months
- 4 months
- 6 months
- 9 months
- 12 months
- 15 months

- 18 months
- 24 months

In addition to administering any vaccines, your child may need the doctor to check their weight, height, eyes, ears, genitals, overall health, and discuss and developmental milestones your child should be achieving and address any concerns you may have.

Once your child has reached the age of two, they should return to the doctor annually for a checkup regardless of if they are due for immunization or not.

In many cases, when your child is sick, over-the-counter remedies, rest, and TLC from a parent can make them feel better; however, when in doubt, it is always OK to call your child's pediatrician to discuss their symptoms.

There are some situations, though, that will require a trip to the doctor. These include:

- A high, persistent fever (typically over 102 for several days)
  - For a newborn under two months, any temperature above 100.4 requires medical attention
- Any breathing problem
- Persistent pain such as a sore throat, earache, stomachache, or headache
- Goopy, yellow, or green eye discharge that does not go away as the day progresses

Frequent vomiting or diarrhea that results in:

- Not producing urine every 6-8 hours
- Vomit or diarrhea contains blood
- Stiff neck, extreme lethargy, or an illness that is not getting better after 4 or 5 days
- Urinary Problems
- If you know, they have been exposed to a contagious disease

Chapter Four Quiz A

1. A fever for a newborn that requires medical attention is anything above:
   a. 100.4
   b. 100
   c. 102
   d. 99.5
2. True or False: Your child does not need to see the doctor for a checkup unless they are due for an immunization.
3. For which of the following conditions should your child see the doctor? Select all that apply.
   a. Yellow or green eye discharge
   b. A runny nose and cough
   c. A low fever (101) for one day
   d. Urinary problems

Dental & Eye Doctor Visits

In addition to regular checkups with the pediatrician, your child should also receive routine care from a dentist and optometrist. While a pediatrician will do a cursory check of your child's mouth and eyes as part of their annual physical, it is essential to take them to see dental and eye professionals for an in-depth evaluation.

Children should visit the dentist for the first time around six months of age or when their first tooth pops up. Of course, this will not be a complete dental exam, but the dentist will be able to make sure your child's mouth and teeth are developing healthily. A visit to the dentist also helps your child become comfortable in the space. After the age of two, your child should visit the dentist every six months.

It is recommended that you start brushing your child's gums with a bristled finger brush or a damp washcloth. This gentle rubbing will help remove bacteria from their mouth. Once teeth start erupting, you can use a small, grain-sized amount of a child's fluoridated toothpaste. Do not let your child swallow the toothpaste. If they frequently try to eat it or swallow it talk to your dentist about other toothpaste options.

For children 3-6, you can use a pea-sized amount of toothpaste. Children this age can brush their teeth themselves but should still be supervised by an adult. Be sure to use a child-sized brush that has soft bristles. You can play games with counting and singing or purchase a timer with lights or music to make it fun and to make sure they are brushing their teeth long enough.

Most children lose their first tooth between the ages of 5-7, but it can happen as early as four and as old as eight.

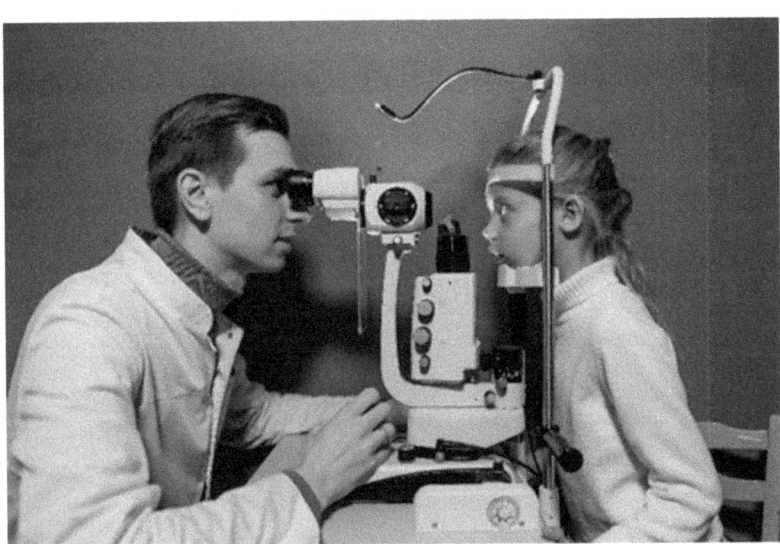

The other specialist, your child, should visit is the optometrist or eye doctor. Many young children struggle in school because of eye problems that are never diagnosed. Eye problems can lead to poor performance in school as well as behavioral problems.

If your child has no diagnosed eye problems or is not complaining of headaches or difficulty reading or seeing, an eye exam every two years is recommended. If they wear glasses or have a vision problem, they should visit annually.

It is recommended for a child to have their first eye doctor visit at six months, then again at the age of 3, and then age 5 or 6 before they begin Kindergarten.

Chapter Four Quiz B

1. True or False: It is ok if your child swallows toothpaste from time to time, as long as it is not a lot.
2. True or False: A child's toothpaste should have firm, stiff bristles to ensure proper teeth cleaning.
3. How often should a child see the optometrist?
   a. Annually
   b. Once every Three Years
   c. Every Two years
   d. Annually if they have an eye issue, every two years if not
4. True or False: Poor eyesight can lead to behavioral problems and difficulty learning in school.

QUIZ B ANSWER GUIDE

1: False. 2: False. 3: D. 4: True.

Germs & Sanitation

Keeping your home and your child's clothing and toys clean is an integral part of keeping your child healthy. Since young children explore by putting things in their mouth, your child's toys should be washed and sanitized regularly.

Never take a toy away from a child while using it, but once they set it down, place it in a plastic bin or mesh bag to wash. Wash the toys with soap and water or run them through your dishwasher using the sanitize setting. If you do not have a dishwasher or sanitize option after washing them by hand, allow them to air dry. If you allow them to dry in the sun, sunlight works as a natural sanitizer. You can also purchase toy safe sanitation sprays to use.

You should also clean and sanitize highchairs, swings, crib slats, strollers, and eating surfaces on a regular basis.

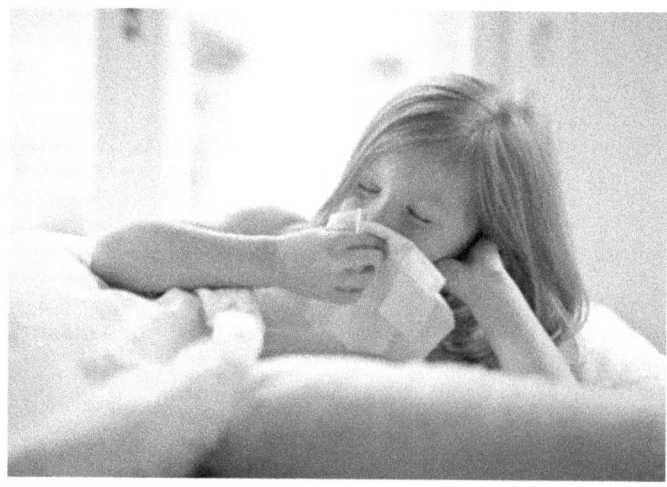

For older children who do not place toys in their mouths, weekly or bi-weekly cleaning should be adequate unless they are sick. When a child is sick, anything they have played with during the last 48 hours should be cleaned as a precaution.

Children are not the best at washing their hands, so it is imperative to clean their items if they are sick.

You should be demonstrating and teaching your child proper handwashing techniques.

Children should wash hand when they come in from outside, home from school, before and after eating, after using the toilet, and after using a tissue to sneeze or blow their nose.

1. Turn on the water
2. Get hands wet
3. 1 or 2 pumps of soap
4. Scrub – AWAY from the water for 20 seconds
   o They can count to twenty or sing ABCs or Happy Birthday twice
   o Encourage them to make their hands covered in bubbles
   o They should wash between their fingers, tops and bottoms, and their wrists
5. Rinse soap off
6. Dry hands
7. Turn off water with a clean towel

Bedding, clothing, and towels should also be washed regularly to maintain good hygiene. Young children do not need to bathe every day unless they have gotten sweaty or dirty, but as they approach the tween and teen years, they should bathe on an almost daily basis.

Children can become resistant to bathing and hygiene, merely because it takes time away from things they enjoy so take the time to teach your child about why hygiene is important and how it keeps them healthy.

Around the age of nine or ten, you should introduce your child to deodorant and discuss body odor and changes like hair growth.

Children should be encouraged to brush their teeth twice daily, brush their hair, and keep their nails clean and trimmed. A lot of bacteria and germs live under fingernails. Consider providing your child with a nail brush if they have difficulty keeping their nails clean.

Proper Nutrition

A child's diet is a significant part of ensuring they grow and develop correctly. Children and teens have specific nutritional needs that should be met. Myplate.gov is an excellent resource for nutritional information. The five food groups that should be included daily are fruits, vegetables, grains, proteins & dairy.

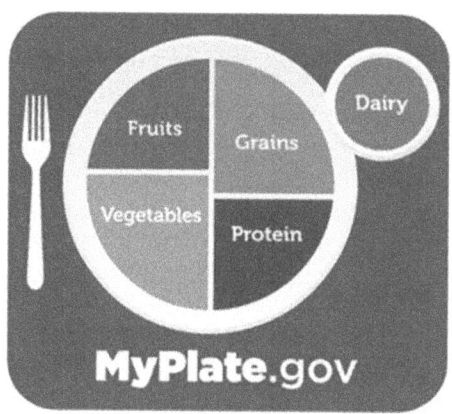

According to MyPlate.gov, half of your child's plate should be made up of fruits and vegetables. A quarter should be whole grains, a quarter protein, and a small serving of low-fat dairy per meal.

Serving sizes vary depending on your child's age. Adults should follow this same system; by doing so, you are setting an example for your child to maintain a healthy diet.

Food	# of Servings Each Day	1-3 Years	4-5 Years	6-12 Years	12 Years +
Grains (bread, cereal, pasta)	5 or less	1/2 slice or 1/4 cup	1/2 slice or 1/2 cup	1 slice or 1/2 cup	1 slice or 1/2 cup
Vegetables	3-5	1/4 cup	1/3 cup	1/2 cup	1/2 cup
Fruits	2-4	1/4 cup	1/3 cup	1/2 cup	1/2 cup
Dairy (milk products)	2-3	1/2 cup	3/4 cup	1 cup	1 cup
Protein	2-3	1 oz. or 1/4 cup	1 1/2 ozs. or 1/3 cup	2 ozs. or 1/2 cup	2-3 ozs. or 1/2 cup

Graphics Courtesy of childrenshealth

Ways to Encourage Healthy Eating

- Include your child in meal prep
- Take them grocery shopping with you

- Eat healthily in front of them
- Read books about food and nutrition
- Do not force your child to eat everything on their plate; instead, encourage them to at least try everything with a "no thank you bite."
  - Forcing children to finish food can result in eating disorders and an unhealthy relationship with food
- NEVER use food as a reward or punishment. Food is there to provide sustenance.
  - This can cause an unhealthy relationship with food to develop.
- If your child refuses to eat what has been prepared (especially if you know it is a food they eat and like), DO NOT make them something different and DO NOT let them fill up on junk food or snacks if they refuse to eat.
  - This is different than forcing them to eat. Do not require them to sit at the table or punish them for not eating. Instead, let them know that this is what is being served and will be here for them when they are ready to eat.
  - Children will not starve themselves; when they are hungry, they will eat.
  - Save the plate and let them know that the plate will be available to them when they are hungry again.
  - The plate of uneaten food does not carry over to the next day. A new day offers a new chance!
- Prepare food in a variety of ways.
  - Mix vegetables into other dishes
  - Season food in different ways
  - Try baked, boiled, or sauteed veggies
  - Serve veggies raw or cooked meat with dip or hummus
  - Use honey, PB, or Nutella to dip fruit in
  - Cook whole grain pasta or veggie infused pasta

Reflective Questions

1. What obstacles stand in the way of you preparing healthy and nutritious food for your child? If you have obstacles, how could you overcome them?

_____

_____

_____

_____

2. What healthy foods do you most enjoy?

_____

_____

_____

_____

3. What are some ways you could include your child in the meal prep or with grocery shopping?

_____

_____

_____

_____

4. What is one thing you can do to include more healthy foods in your diet?

_____

_____

_____

_____

Children & Exercise

Along with a healthy diet, children need to engage in regular physical activity. Children do not need to be engaged in any formal exercise program; running, jumping, and playing will do! Of course, if they play an organized sport, do yoga with you, or enjoy nature walks, that counts too!

Toddlers and preschoolers should be active several times a day and have at least one to two hours of active play daily .

School-age children should have a minimum of one hour of play a day.

Active play should include activities that work both large and small muscles and include climbing, running, skipping, jumping, crawling, balls, hand-eye coordination, and strength building.

If you do not have a lot of outside space, you can dance to music in your house, do yoga and stretching, and find kid-friendly workout videos online.

Exercise is not just the "healthy" thing to do; children's bodies need physical movement and activity to grow and develop their brain, muscles, and bones. When planning activities for your child, keep in mind these three things: endurance, flexibility, and strength.

Children should be limited to 1-2 hours of passive screen time a day. Passive screen time includes watching videos, movies, and television.

It is important that your children see you be active as well. If you make exercise a priority, they will want to be active too! Children mimic what they see adults do.

Physical Activities to do With Your Child

- Go for a walk
- Go for a bike ride
- Take the dog for a walk
- Take a neighborhood scavenger hunt (lists can be found online)
- Play tag
- Jump rope
- Play hopscotch
- Do a bean bag toss
- Kick or throw a ball back and forth
- Go swimming
- Do yoga together
- Dance together
- Go ice skating
- Have them chase bubbles
- Turn on the sprinkler and run around together in bathing suits
- Learn a new sport together
- Play in the snow
- Play tennis or ping pong
- Go bowling
- Go mini golfing
- Go to the batting cages

Reflective Questions

1. Are exercise and fitness important to you? Why or why not?

_____

_____

_____

_____

2. What is one way you could add more activity to your child's day?

_____

_____

_____

_____

3. What is a physical activity you enjoy? Why do you enjoy doing it? How could you involve your child?

_____

_____

Chapter Four Quiz C

1. How much physical activity does a toddler or preschooler need daily?
   a. 30 minutes
   b. 1-2 hours
   c. 2-3 hours
   d. 45 minutes
2. What are the three things to keep in mind when planning physical activity for a child?
   a. Dexterity, flexibility, endurance
   b. Flexibility, accuracy, strength
   c. Endurance, flexibility, strength
   d. Accuracy, endurance, strength
3. True or False: A child needs physical activity for their body and brain to develop.
4. True or False: If you are engaged in physical activity, your children are likely to want to do it too.

QUIZ C ANSWER GUIDE

1: B. 2: C. 3: True. 4: True.

Substance Abuse

Children exposed to substance abuse are more likely to experience behavioral problems, perform poorly in school, engage in violent and risky behavior, engage in early sexual experimentation, run away, and experiment with drugs and alcohol themselves.

Even if you are not the person with the substance abuse problem, allowing anyone into your home that suffers from an addiction can have adverse effects on your child's mental well-being and development.

Cases of children being removed from their homes due to a parent with a substance abuse problem have risen dramatically. In 2000 roughly 18% percent of cases were due to substance abuse; by 2016, it rose to 35%.

If you have a substance abuse problem, it is crucial for your health and your child's well-being to seek professional help.

Tobacco use is the most prevalent drug in use, and while it is legal to smoke cigarettes second-hand smoke is dangerous to the child and can produce long-term effects. If you do smoke, keep it out of the home and away from your children. Never allow anyone else to smoke near your children, either.

Alcohol abuse followed by illicit drug use are the next two most commonly abused.

Parents who engage in the regular use of illegal drugs or drink too much are less effective at parenting due to the brain impairment caused by the drug. Critical thinking skills are impaired, as well as gross and fine motor skills.

There is also a strong link between substance abuse and child abuse and neglect. Parents who are addicted have impaired judgment and may accidentally injure and forget about their child. For some people, drug and alcohol use makes them angry, irritable, and more likely to last out.

Resources for Addiction and Substance Abuse

If you or a loved one need substance abuse help, start by contacting one of the resources below.

American Addiction Centers – (888) 257-1594

SmartRecovery.org – (440) 951-5357

Alcoholics Anonymous AA.org

National Drug Helpline – 1-844-289-0879

Reflective Questions

1. Has alcohol or drug use impaired or affected your ability to parent?

_____

_____

_____

_____

_____

2. If you answered yes above, what are your motivations for drug or alcohol use?

_____

_____

_____

_____

_____

_____

3. What steps do you need to take to seek help for yourself or another adult in your child's life?

_____

_____

_____

_____

_____

_____

4. What are some things you can do to help curb urges you may have?

_____

_____

_____

_____

_____

_____

Chapter Five
Discipline

What is Discipline?

Discipline is often a hot-button topic when it comes to parenting. Everyone from our mothers to our best friends and even the random person in the grocery store seems to have a comment on how you should be handling your child's behavior. The long and short of it is, if you are not abusing your child or causing them harm emotionally, physically, or sexually, it is honestly no one else's business how you discipline your child. That being said, some methods are more effective than others and will produce better results in the long run, resulting in a happier and healthier child and a less stressed-out parent.

So, what exactly is discipline? By definition, Discipline is a method of teaching to correct someone's behavior. The root of the word is discipulus which is Latin for pupil or student. We often use the word discipline to mean punishment, when in reality, we should be using it to mean teaching.

When discipline is used effectively, it reduces punishment because children are treated with value and respect in place of shame and degradation. Effective discipline involves teaching children how to fix their mistakes, understand the emotions behind their actions, make better choices, and when appropriate consequences; some natural, some enforced.

Discipline should not include berating, shaming, humiliation, teasing, lengthy time-outs or separation, or any type of physical punishment, including spanking. Repeated studies have shown the harmfulness of spanking on a child's emotional development, not to mention it is not an effective form of discipline. Punishments and discipline that teach children to fear rather than change their behavior and make better choices do nothing to benefit their development and growth.

Reflective Questions

1. What are the main types of discipline you commonly use in your home currently?

_____

_____

_____

_____

_____

_____

2. Do you use time-outs? Are they effective? Why or why not?

_____

_____

_____

_____

3. What changes would you like to make in your discipline style?

_____

_____

_____

_____

The Negative Side Effects of Spanking

Spanking has been proven to have a multitude of adverse side effects for children. Chief among them, children who are spanked often have aggression issues, slowed cognitive development, trust issues, negative effects on the parent-child relationship, and often makes a child's behavior worse.

Think of it this way. Suppose a parent is mad at their child for drawing on the wall; what parent would not be upset? What does the upset parent do? They grab their child and smack them hard on the bottom and say, "We don't color on the wall!" The message just sent to that small child is, "When a person is angry, it is ok to hit someone."

So, the next time the child is playing with a sibling or friend and becomes angry, they hit the other child. Likely, they will get in trouble for hitting, the same thing a parent did to them when the parent was angry! Their brain goes, "Well, that's not fair!" The child becomes confused, upset and does not know what is right or wrong because no one took the time to explain it to them.

Now imagine this scenario instead. The parent sees the child drew on the wall, and when they are calm, they call the child ad goes to them. They point at the wall and say, "I am very upset right now; you colored on the wall, that damages the wall. Where are you supposed to color?" The child may be quiet because they know they are in trouble, or they may speak up and say, "On paper." The parent says, "Yes, on paper. I need you to help me clean this up, and if you color on the walls again, you will lose your crayons for two days."

In the second scenario, the child still receives a consequence, having to help clean; they also understand that their parent is upset and that they made a mistake. The correct behavior is reinforced. The child is also given an ultimatum on what will happen if they make the same mistake again.

Numerous studies have found that spanking increases the likelihood of a child developing depression, anxiety, low self-esteem, increased aggression, and other delinquent behaviors.

Spanking does nothing to teach a child what they did wrong; there is no connection between their action and the parent's response. When children misbehave, they are often seeking attention or some form of connection with the parent or caregiver. When you spank a child, you are further damaging that connection, leading to more behavioral problems.

Spanking often makes you feel worse as a parent. Almost all parents have felt that visceral gut reaction to spank their child. It is a chemical reaction to anger and a child's out-of-control behavior, but once your brain and body are balanced back out, you realize spanking is the wrong course of action. When we spank, it affects our self-esteem and worth as parents, and we often feel guilty afterward.

The rest of the chapter will deal with more effective and beneficial discipline styles to help you and your child.

Reflective Questions

1. Do you spank or smack your children's hands or use any other type of physical punishment? Why?

_____

_____

_____

_____

_____

2. If you answered yes above, how do you feel after you've spanked your child?

_____

_____

_____

3. Describe why experts believe spanking is an ineffective form of punishment:

_____

_____

_____

Positive Discipline

The phrase positive discipline may seem incongruent to you; how on earth could discipline be positive? Positive discipline means that guidelines, rules, rewards, and consequences are clearly laid out and taught so that a child understands the benefits of following the rules or consequences of not doing so.

Psychologist Jane Nelsen developed the phrase Positive Discipline. She created an entire system around treating children with respect and parents working as coaches to guide their children to the correct behavior.

Positive discipline does not mean kids do whatever they want; it does not mean there are never consequences, and it does not mean parents are pushovers.

Positive discipline is centered on encouraging the behavior you want to see and ignoring that you don't. Children crave and need attention, and if they learn that the only way they can get it is through negative behaviors, then that is what they will do.

Think of a situation where your child did what they were asked, for example, putting their toys away. Chances are you didn't make a big deal about it, aka, little to no reaction. Now, what about the last time your child misbehaved? You might have shouted, scolded, and showed agitation, aka a big reaction.

Now imagine flip-flopping the two and giving your child a huge, exciting, and happy reaction when they did what was expected and a very calm flat reaction when they misbehave. Over time your child will seek out positive attention because it is bigger; it fills their attention need better.

You may balk at this and think, "I'm not throwing my kid a parade for doing what they're expected to do," yet that is precisely what you should be doing. Positive, happy reactions are your child's currency for doing their job correctly. When you perform your job correctly, you get a paycheck and hopefully positive feedback from your boss, children need a form of payment, too, and the best method is through positive reactions to their positive choices. If you got paid more when you gave 100% versus when you gave 75% chances, you're going to give 100% more often than not.

Positive Discipline is also about empowering your child with choices. Children have very little control over their world; they are often told what to do and when to do it; lack of power and control leads to frustration, leading to misbehavior. It would be best to find the opportunities to empower your child through daily, realistic, choices; the keyword being realistic.

A realistic choice would be, "Do you want to wear the green shirt or the purple shirt today? We need to leave for school, and it's up for you to decide."

An unrealistic choice would be, "If you don't pick a shirt in the next two minutes, you're going to school without one." Why is it unrealistic? Because you cannot follow through. You can't send your kid to school with no shirt on, so you've already lost the battle.

If you need to set a limit because the clock is ticking, then it becomes, "Do you want to wear the green shirt or the purple shirt today? We need to leave for school. I am giving you three more minutes to choose, and then the choice becomes mine. You have the choice right now, so make a decision." Set a timer and walk away. You put the ball in their court and gave them the power.

Here's another example, "You can clean your toys up before bath or after bath, but if they are not cleaned up before bedtime anything left out you lose for the next three days." Simple, to the point, and leaves no room for misunderstanding.

Giving them choices gives them back some control, which will make them more compliant and better behaved. You force them to decide with a clear understanding of the outcome if they don't, thus teaching them accountability for their actions.

Tips & Tricks

- When your child acts aggressively, kicks, hits, bites, calmly and firmly, tell them that it is not ok to hurt someone. If they are old enough, ask them what made them so upset? Then say, let's think of words or actions we can do instead of hurting someone.
- Offer them realistic choices throughout the day. Be sure you can follow through on the choice.
- Set up expectations and consequences ahead of time so there is no misunderstanding.
  - If needed, give a warning the first time, then state what will happen if they make the same choice again.
- Talk to your child about their feelings. Discover their motivation for certain behaviors and find alternatives. i.e., they didn't do their math homework because it was hard, so you schedule time each night to help them or set them up with a tutor.
- Follow through on consequences. If you say they will lose their Xbox for a week if they don't do their homework again, take the Xbox away if they fail to turn in their work.
- Use natural consequences when possible. i.e., "You have 10 minutes until we need to leave for the party; if your room is still not cleaned up, we are not leaving, and you will be late."
- Support them with positive praise, "Your room has stayed clean all week; I think you earned 15 extra minutes of tablet time!"

Reflective Questions

1. What do you think are your biggest hurdles in trying positive discipline?

_____

_____

_____

_____

2. What are some realistic choices you can offer your child right away?

_____

_____

_____

_____

3. List three things daily you can praise your child for doing.

_____

_____

_____

_____

Chapter 5 Quiz A

1. True or False: Children need attention, so they will seek out any attention they can get, whether negative or positive.
2. True or False: Talking about emotions with children is pointless because they are too young to understand.
3. True or False: Praise and clear expectations are the best methods to get your children to follow directions.
4. True or False: Offering realistic choices daily to your child is a way to empower them.

QUIZ A ANSWER GUIDE

1: True. 2: False. 3: True. 4: True

Time Outs

Time out is a common phrase in parenting, but very few people actually know what a time out really is or how to use them properly.

Time-outs should be used sparingly and as a method to calm the child down, not as a punishment where a child is expected to sit perfectly still and quiet.

Time-outs are most effective between the ages of two and five or six when your child has some facets of self-control. A time-out should be one minute for each year of your child's age.

You should have a designated spot for time-outs and use the same spot each time.

Explain to your child that the time out is a time for them to calm their body down and create calm thoughts.

Once the timer is over, get down on your child's level and repeat what the time out was for, "You hit your brother you sat in time out for 3 minutes. Ask them what they should do differently next time or how they could fix the problem, then allow them to return to the situation.

Rewards and Incentives

Children love rewards, and, in some cases, the best or only way to get a child to comply or behave in a specific way is through a reward and incentive program. Children are still learning right from wrong, so the moral compass that guides adults is not always there to keep them on track. Adults feel an intrinsic or internal motivation to do the right thing; children often need extrinsic or outward motivation.

When reward charts are used effectively, they can be a great tool to aid in parenting. Some situations that may require a reward system are getting ready for bed, brushing teeth, keeping their room clean, getting ready for school in the morning, or following directions the first time they are asked.

Let's suppose your child presents the biggest behavioral challenge at bedtime. You can create a reward chart on which your child can receive a sticker if they can get their pajamas on, brush their teeth, and be in bed with a book picked out in 15 minutes or less. Each time they meet that goal, they get a sticker. Once they earn five stickers, they can choose a prize.

Prizes could be small toys you keep in a bin, an extra story at bedtime, or extra time on the tablet or TV. Prizes should NEVER be food. Using food as a reward sets up an unhealthy relationship with food.

As time goes on, increase the number of stickers they need to earn the prize. An example of a reward schedule is:

- ✓ 5 Stickers
- ✓ 5 Stickers
- ✓ 7 Stickers
- ✓ 10 Stickers
- ✓ 10 Stickers

- ✓ 15 Stickers
- ✓ 20 Stickers

Eventually, they won't need the sticker incentive because the behavior will now be a habit. Prizes can also grow. One prize might be they get to choose a particular activity to do with mom or dad. In this case, if they pick to get ice cream or eat at a favorite fast food restaurant, then food is ok because, in this situation, the incentive wasn't the food; the incentive was time with their parent.

When using a reward chart, avoid using charts with the days of the week on them. No one's entire week should be blown because they missed one day of making the right choices. Instead, use charts that have blocks of five or ten squares. If a child doesn't earn a sticker, leave that square blank for the next day. The goal should be to earn a specific number of stickers or marks, not achieve perfection seven days a week.

For older children, money, time with friends, and freedom from chores are three very effective incentives. You probably won't need a reward chart with an older child, but establishing guidelines for the incentive is important. For example, if the goal is to bring their grades up, you can agree on a set amount for each A or B on their report card.

An example grade schedule is:

- ✓ $5 for each A
- ✓ $2 for each B
- ✓ $0 for each C
- ✓ $-2 for each D
- ✓ $-5 for each F

Whatever you agree upon with an older child, put it in writing and save it that way; there are no discrepancies later. Older children are likely to look for loopholes, so if your agreement is in writing, there will be no confusion or argument over the finer details. You can even make it a formal "contract" by having each of you sign the document.

Emotional Intelligence

According to Cambridge Dictionary, the definition of emotional intelligence is:

The ability to understand the way people feel and react and to use this skill to make good judgments and to avoid or solve problems.

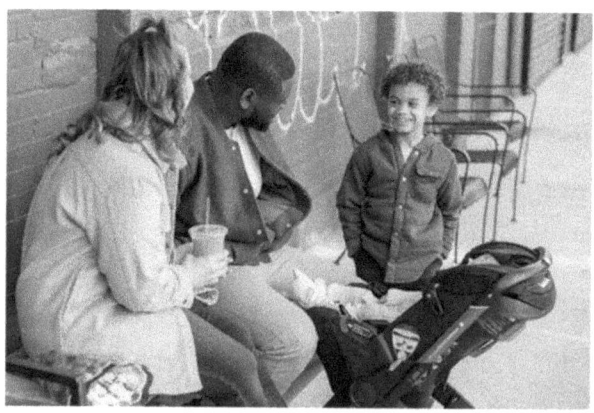

The ability to understand and control your own feelings and to understand the feelings of others and react to them in a suitable way.

To put it in simple terms, people who possess emotional intelligence are able to handle and process their emotions effectively. They are able to better interact with others, show empathy, and can feel sympathy for others.

Much of a child's emotional intelligence is developed by their interactions with their parents and other adult role models. A child who is able to develop strong emotional intelligence has more confidence and self-awareness. They can express their emotions effectively, which reduces tantrums and misbehavior.

Children with strong emotional intelligence perform better in school because they can focus on academics when their emotions are in check.

Talk about your emotions with your child. Share with them things that make you happy, excited, nervous, scared, angry, etc.

Ask your child about their feelings in different situations. If their emotions are overly intense, talk about ways to handle strong emotions, such as going for a walk, writing about it, taking some time alone, or hugging a stuffed animal.

The more transparent you can be with your emotions and the more you can create a safe environment to express emotions, the more it will help your child.

Tips to Help Your Child Develop Emotional Intelligence

- Read books with your children in which the characters have strong feelings
- Practice breathing exercises with your child
    - Count backward slowly from 1-5 as you breathe in through your nose and out through your mouth
    - Have your child imagine they are holding a cupcake with a candle. Pretend to smell the cupcake together and then slowly blow the candle out
    - Lie down on your back with your hands on your belly on the floor and count up to 10
- Ask "What If" questions to provide your child a chance to think about how they would handle a situation.
    - What would you do if someone fell and start crying?
    - What would you do if someone took a toy that wasn't theirs?
    - What would you do if you felt very angry?
- Do Yoga together
- Have your child bend down and touch their toes. When you invert your body and get your head below your heart, your body naturally fights against the cortisol produced when stressed.

Parent Self Care

One of the best ways to be an effective parent is to take care of yourself. When you maintain your identity as an adult, have hobbies and interests outside of parenting and housework, and see or speak with friends regularly, you are better emotionally equipped to deal with parenting stressors.

It is essential that you find other adults you can lean on when parenting becomes stressful. Even if it is someone just to talk to on the phone, a support system is key.

Regular exercise is also important. Exercise naturally relieves stress and helps you sleep better. Getting regular sleep makes a big difference in your ability to parent as well. If you are not adequately rested, you will be tired and likely have a shorter temper.

Find a hobby, preferably one that gets you outside of the house once in a while. Consider joining a book club, playing a team sport, auditioning for a community theater production, or attend a weekly spin class.

If getting out of the home is not possible, you could take up gardening, work on puzzles, read, learn how to knit or sew, etc.

Parents, moms especially, need to break the mindset that self-care is indulgent or selfish. Parents are people too!

Other ways to take care of yourself include home spa treatments or getting your nails done regularly, or a weekly coffee date with a friend. If you are in a relationship, you and your partner should plan regular date nights to focus on yourself as a couple.

When you, as a parent, are constantly trying to meet the needs of everyone else in the family and ignoring yourself, you are doing more harm than good. Your family will feel the stress you are experiencing as well.

Things to Try

- Make a homemade foot scrub and give yourself a pedicure
- Buy yourself flowers
- Make a cup of tea and read a book
- Go for a walk and enjoy nature
- Call a friend and meet up for lunch
- Join a virtual yoga class
- Meditate
- Listen to music
- Start a gratitude journal
- Spend time alone
- Tackle some things on your to-do list
- Buy yourself a small treat like a new pair of shoes or a book you've wanted

Reflective Questions

1. What are some things you enjoy you wish you had more time to do?

_____

_____

_____

_____

2. What needs to happen for you to be able to carve out more time for yourself?

_____

_____

_____

_____

3. List three ways you are going to practice self-care this month:

_____

_____

_____

_____

4. What is one new thing you would like to try?

_____

_____

_____

_____

Anger Management

Feeling anger is entirely natural for a parent. Our children have ways of pushing our buttons like no one else. It can even feel frightening at times how angry you can feel at your child. What is important is how you handle that anger.

The first step in handling your anger is learning to understand it. Think about your relationship with anger. Were you taught anger is bad? Did you have a parent who was often angry, and is it how you learned to express yourself?

Anger is neither good nor bad; it is a feeling like any other. Feeling anger is just as normal and ok as feeling happiness.

The Center for Parenting Education advises you to look at your anger like a tree.

Like a tree, anger has:

- roots (the underlying causes),
- a trunk (your expression of anger),
- fruit (the results of your anger, which can begin a new anger tree).

To help manage your anger, begin to recognize the physical signs in your body. Do you become hot? Do you tense your muscles or grit your teeth? Do you feel short of breath? Can you feel your heartbeat go faster?

Next, you need to force yourself to calm down. You can do this in many ways. It may be walking away from the child and isolating yourself in the bedroom for a bit. You may need to do some deep breathing or go for a walk.

It takes at least twenty minutes for your body to process the fight or flight reaction when you become angered. If needed, take that time to ground yourself psychologically and prepare yourself to handle the situation that angered you.

Take time to figure out what is at the root of your anger in the situation. Is it your child's behavior? Do you have unmet needs (you slept poorly, you haven't eaten all afternoon, your friend canceled your much-needed night out last night, etc.)? Do you have underlying emotions surrounding the situation (your son knocked over and broke your favorite coffee mug that you've had since college, you struggled with math in school, and now your child is not doing their math homework, etc.).

When speaking to your child use "I" statements to express your feelings. Stick to the facts and do not shame your child or place blame. "When you refuse to brush your teeth, I become very frustrated", "When you are not handing in your homework it upsets me because I know you are not trying your hardest." These statements clearly outline what you are feeling and why without shaming your child or using derogatory statements.

There are three parts to an "I" Statement:

- I feel (angry)
- When I see/hear (you have skipped school)
- Because (I know how important good grades are to future success)

If you lost your temper, then apologize to your child for losing your temper; do not apologize for being angry. "I am sorry I yelled so loudly, that wasn't the right way to talk to you, but I feel angry and not respected when I see you still watching TV because I have asked you three times to get dressed for school."

Reflective Questions

1. What are some things that trigger your anger?

_____

_____

_____

_____

2. What are some techniques you currently use to calm down?

_____

_____

_____

_____

3. Think of a recent situation in which your child angered you. Now write out an "I" statement you could use to express your feelings in that situation.

_____

_____

_____

_____

Chapter 5 Quiz B

1. How long does it take for your body to calm down from the fight or flight response?
    a. 15 minutes
    b. 10 minutes
    c. 25 minutes
    d. 20 minutes
2. If you are thinking of anger as a tree, what does the trunk represent?
    a. The results of your anger
    b. The way you express your anger
    c. The cause of your anger
    d. Staying steady and not expressing anger
3. True of False: Using "I" Statements are an effective way to express your feelings
4. True or False: Understanding the root cause of your anger or frustration is an important part of processing it.

QUIZ B ANSWER KEY

1: D. 2: B. 3: True. 4: True.

Chapter Six
Consistency

Consistency is Important

Consistency in parenting is vital to your success as a parent. When parents are consistent in their behaviors, rules, discipline, and feedback children, know what to expect. When children know what to expect, they are less anxious, have less stress, and few behavioral problems. A child's life is made up of internalizing, rehearsing, and repeating.

To help you picture why consistency is important, imagine you have an unpredictable boss at work. One day they criticize and yell at you for even the smallest of errors, and the next, the same mistake gets no response. This same boss never provides clear instructions on how they'd like the work done, so you always have to guess to get it right. Can you feel how stressful that would be?

It is the same for children. They put all their trust in the adults around them, and if the adults are not consistent, the child feels stress and confusion. They do not know what is expected of them because it has never been clearly outlined.

Children require consistent and clear guidelines and expectations for their behavior. You need to focus on what they can do as opposed to what they cannot. Children respond better to positive directions. Positive phrasing is beneficial for adults as it allows for more transparent communication.

Keep in mind; consistency doesn't mean inflexibility. With young children, you have to be able to adapt to change quickly and be flexible at times. Surprises come up, and children are definitely full of surprises.

You may realize that a rule you've made is too rigid or that a consequence you set is too harsh or not realistic. If that is the case, then explain to your child why you are making the change. Adapting from time to time shows your child that, at times, changes are needed and that it is ok to do so for the right reasons. Just be careful not to give in to every argument your child makes, or inconsistency will reign again.

Reflective Questions

1. In what areas of your life do you feel you are consistent? What makes it easy to be consistent?

_____

_____

_____

_____

2. In what areas of your life do you lack consistency? Why? How could you change that?

_____

_____

_____

_____

How to Set Limits, Rules, & Expectations

Setting limits is a significant part of being consistent. As mentioned in the introduction to the chapter, if a child doesn't know what is expected of them, how can they possibly know how to behave? Think of your favorite game. Are their rules? The assumption is yes because, without rules, no one knows what is allowed or how to play. It is important to establish the rules in your home, so your child knows what to do.

Setting limits is as easy as 1, 2, 3

1. **State the expectation:** You are required to be home at 10 pm on Friday.
2. **State the consequence if the expectation is not met:** If you are not home by 10 pm, you will be grounded for the next two weekends.
3. Have your child repeat the expectation and the consequence back to you.

For younger children, you may need to repeat the same guideline repeatedly each time it comes up.

1. **State the expectation:** Remember the rule is you have to brush your teeth the first time.
2. **State the consequence if the expectation is not met:** If you don't brush your teeth the first time I ask, you will lose one of your stories tonight.
3. Have your child repeat the expectation and the consequence back to you.

Young children, especially those who cannot read, will benefit from a picture schedule to help them through the day. These can be pictures you take of them performing their day's various actions, or you could print them from a computer.

When setting expectations for your child, they need to be realistic and something your child can realistically do. If your four-year-old has taken every piece of clothing out of their dresser and thrown them all over the room, it would not be realistic to expect them to fold it all and put it back. What would be realistic is that you sit with them, teach them how to fold, and make them help put the clothes back neatly.

Similarly, if your teen struggles with math and seeks out additional help such as a tutor or extra credit, it would not be realistic to say they have to earn an A or have a consequence. What would be realistic is bringing a D grade up to a C or a B for the next marking period.

Consequences & Follow-Through

The follow-up to setting limits and expectations is follow-through. If you do not follow through on a consequence, your child knows there is no reason to follow the rule. It is not easy to watch your child cry because they lost a favorite toy or failed the test and are grounded for the weekend and cry they will. Expect your child to tell you they hate you, that you are mean, and they wish they had a different parent. Your job is not to be your child's friend; it is to love, teach, and guide them to become successful and healthy adults.

At the same time, consequences and follow-through are not about being unkind or upsetting your child; it teaches your child that rules and expectations need to be followed. Remember not to use consequences to shame or blame your child; they should be used to teach.

After a negative interaction with your child, follow up as soon as appropriate with a positive interaction. This helps re-establish the trust and bond your child has with you. It can be something as simple as, "Hey, I noticed you put all your laundry in the basket today; thank you, that's really awesome." Or "Do you want to play a game of Candy Land together?"

To be successful with setting limits and consequences, you need to set realistic consequences. Think of the age-old "If you don't quiet down right now, I'm turning this car around right now!" Will you? Are you truly willing to turn the car around? If not, then don't offer it as a possibility.

It bears repeating: If you are unwilling to follow through, then do not offer a consequence. If you say you will leave the store if they don't stop grabbing groceries off the shelf, be prepared to leave a cart full of groceries and leave the store. If you tell your teen they will lose their phone if they fail to turn in their homework, then you better be ready for wailing and gnashing of teeth when you take their phone away.

If consequences are not carried out, your child will quickly learn that you aren't serious and have no reason to follow whatever rule or expectation you are setting.

Additionally, consequences need to be related to the rule. Taking away their iPad for throwing food at the dinner table does not correspond. Making your child clean up all the food they throw and then washing the dishes is an appropriate and related consequence.

Consequences for younger children need to be immediate; young children live in the here and now. Another old adage, "Wait till your father gets home," is not effective because by the time "their father" gets home, their action is so far removed that a child is either one, no longer even remembering what they did, or has been instilled with fear which means that the punishment their expecting is probably harsh and brutal and may even be child abuse.

When your child misbehaves, and it is a situation where a guideline hasn't previously been established, you need to immediately issue a warning and state what will happen if the behavior happens again.

"If you hit your sister again, you will be playing by yourself in your room for the next hour." Then, if they hit again, follow through and have them play in their room for an hour.

For older children and teens, the consequence can be longer or slightly delayed. For example, "If your room is not cleaned up by Friday night, you will not be going to the Football game with your friends," or "If you fail to turn in your homework this week, you will lose your PlayStation for the weekend."

Hosting regular family meetings is an excellent way to discuss current rules and introduce new ones. It provides a neutral space for everyone's voice to be heard.

Family meetings need to be held regularly to be effective. A suggested schedule might be twice a month or every week on the same day and same time.

During a family meeting, electronics and phones should be put away. Everyone should have the opportunity to speak if they wish, but only one person at a time should be speaking. You can use a token to hold for younger children, such as a wand or speaking stick. Whoever is holding the speaking stick is the only person allowed to talk.

As a parent, you should encourage your child to ask questions about new rules or guidelines. This doesn't mean you allow rules to be ignored or fought, but it does show your children you respect them and are willing to listen to their opinions and ideas.

Reflective Questions

1. What are some of the known rules or expectations in your home?

_____

_____

_____

_____

_____

2. Do the known rules and expectations have consistent consequences?

_____

_____

_____

_____

3. What are some new rules or expectations you'd like to see in your home?

_____

_____

_____

_____

4. Do you have family meetings? If so, how regularly? What are the rules of the meeting? If not, do you plan on starting them? Why or why not?

_____

_____

_____

_____

Chapter 6 Quiz A

1. True or False: Holding a family meeting whenever someone has a problem is the best approach.
2. True or False: Consistency helps children feel secure because they know what to expect.
3. What are the three steps to setting a limit?
   a. Set the expectation, state the consequence if the expectation is not met, have your child repeat the expectation and consequence back to you
   b. Set the expectation, wait until the child has failed to meet the expectation, set a consequence because the expectation was not met
   c. Set the same consequence for all failed expectations, have your child repeat the set consequence back to you, enforce the consequence because they did not meet the expectation
   d. Let your child set the expectation and consequence, have your child repeat the expectation back to you, enforce the consequence because they did not meet the expectation
4. True or False: If you set a consequence, it is essential to follow through and carry out the consequence.
5. True or False: If your child is angry at you for enforcing a consequence, you should feel bad and let them do what they wanted to do.
6. True or False: Consequences for young children need to be immediate; waiting until later in the day will make the consequence lose its effectiveness.
7. Pick the most appropriate consequence for a child who refuses to clean up their toys:

a. Losing their TV time for the next day
b. Going to bed 20 minutes early
c. Having the toys, they refused to clean up taken away for a few days
d. Losing dessert after dinner
8. True or False: Consequences and expectations need to be realistic.
9. Pick the most appropriate consequence for a teen who broke their curfew:
a. Having them take the garbage out for a week
b. Grounding them for the next two weekends
c. Losing their phone for a day
d. Making them do their own laundry for a week
10. True or False: During family meetings, it is ok for people to be on their phones as long as they seem to be listening to what is being said.

QUIZ A ANSWER GUIDE

1: False. 2: True. 3: A. 4: True. 5: False. 6: True 7: C. 8: True. 9: B. 10: False.

Chapter Seven
Social Skills

What are Social Skills?

Social skills are our ability to interact with another person. The better developed a person's social skills, the better able they are able to have productive relationships, meaningful daily interactions, and coping skills when something doesn't go their way.

Social skills are learned skills. While humans are naturally social animals, a person's social skills must be taught, tended, and nurtured by the adults in their lives.

Children who lack social skills are prone to aggression and behavioral problems because they lack the ability to express their emotions or adequately regulate themselves adequately.

Children need to see adults engage in healthy social interactions to learn how to do it themselves. When adults frequently model healthy social interactions, children observe both the language and the tone of voice and body language.

Even when our discussions with other adults are on serious topics or disagreements, we should showcase to our children the proper way to handle strong emotions without yelling and fighting. If we know that a conversation may become heated, it is best to wait and have those discussions away from young children. Children feel insecure and unsafe when the adults around them are fighting even if there are not in any danger from the adults.

One of the best skills we can teach our children is Active Listening. Active Listening shows the other person we are engaged in what they are saying and sends signals that we support them and empathize. Active Listening is especially important when you disagree because it can help everyone stay calm.

How to Be an Active Listner

- Give your full attention
- Use open, relaxed body language
- Don't interrupt; wait until they have finished speaking
- Reflect on what they've said and repeat it back
  - "It sounds like…:
  - "If I'm understanding…."
- Validate their feelings
- Ask questions that show you are listening
- Avoid advice or passing judgment

Reflective Questions

1. What social skills do you feel are your strongest?

_____

_____

_____

_____

2. Which social skills do you find challenging?

_____

_____

_____

_____

3. How do you handle discussions when you disagree with someone?

_____

_____

4. Do you know what active listening is? Do you employ active listening when you are having a difficult conversation?

_____

_____

_____

_____

5. How important are social interactions in your day-to-day life? Do you have to be social for work or school?

_____

_____

_____

_____

6. Do you enjoy being social? Why are why not?

_____

_____

_____

_____

Emotions

Emotions encompass all areas of our lives. Part of raising a healthy child is fostering their emotional development. Children have strong emotions, and intense emotions can be both positive and negative. Children need to be taught how to handle positive emotions as well as negative ones.

When teaching your children about emotions, you must come to grips with your own feelings about emotions. You may have been taught that certain emotions were feminine or masculine or that some were acceptable and others were not. You may have even been raised in a house where emotions weren't talked about or expressed at all.

First, understand that emotions have no gender. It is not weak or girly to cry or be afraid. Boys don't need to toughen up and fight their way through problems. In fact, research has shown that boys who grow up feeling safe expressing their emotions and feelings grow up to be better partners, fathers, and more compassionate to others in general.

In line with emotions, not having genders understand that there are no wrong emotions. All emotions are valid. There are healthy and unhealthy ways to process emotions. There are reactions your child must learn to temper; for example, crying for two hours because their sister ate the last green jolly rancher is not an appropriate reaction; feeling disappointed that the last green jolly rancher is gone is ok.

A famous saying in early childhood settings goes, "You get what you get, and you don't get upset." This saying tells children that they are not allowed to feel negative emotions. Of course, you can be upset if you don't get what you want; that's a natural human emotion; what is important is how we handle that emotion.

The second step in helping your child process their emotions is understanding that you cannot fix everything. As parents, we have the instinct to fix every little problem our children have. Unfortunately, this does not teach our children how to solve their problems or how to face disappointment. You must be there to support your child when they face disappointment but resist the urge to fix everything.

Third, you must communicate with your children. Communicate about what you are feeling, ask them what they are feeling. Maintaining open and honest communication with your child around emotions provides them a safe space to express and explore their feelings.

Positive Emotions

When children are excited and happy, that can translate to anxiety, and anxiety can turn into behavioral problems. This can happen when you're at a birthday party, getting ready for a vacation, waiting for a holiday like Christmas, and other situations that may overstimulate your child.

Plan for these moments by learning your child's cues for anxious excitement or overstimulation. They may ask a lot of questions about the event, talk loudly, have difficulty focusing on other tasks, become clingy, interrupt, or they may become emotional and whiny.

These behaviors can be annoying and frustrating to adults, but it is essential to remember this is how your child is exhibiting their excitement and anxiety.

Pay attention to when and where your child seems to become overly excited often and take notes so that you can search for patterns. Note what time of day, what was happening right before, what other people were around, and what eventually helped your child calm down . These details will help you be able to recognize patterns of behavior more easily. Use this Three R concept to help you Recognize, Read, and Respond to your child. Recognize when your child is getting overexcited, read their cues, and respond in a way that helps your child.

Reflective Questions

1. Are you comfortable expressing your own emotions? Why or why not?

_____

_____

_____

_____

_____

_____

2. Does being around angry or sad people make you feel uncomfortable? Why or what not?

_____

_____

_____

_____

_____

_____

Emotion Activities

Young Children 5 & Under

Sing "If You're Happy and You Know It" and put in as many emotions and actions as you can think of that correspond. For example, "If you're angry, say I need space!" or "If you're sad, ask for a hug."	Make an Emotions Chart using pictures of your child expressing different emotions. Hang it in their room.	Read books with your children about emotions and with characters that express strong emotions.
Roleplay emotions with dolls, puppets, and stuffed animals.	At the end of the night, ask them about their favorite things from the day.	Print off an emotion scale like the one below and laminate it so that your child can reference it. This is helpful for younger children and non-verbal children.

| Awful | Not very good | Okay | Really good | Fantastic |

School-Age Children

Have your child keep a gratitude journal. They can also draw pictures to express what they're grateful for.	Encourage your child to keep a diary to write about emotions. They can also draw pictures to express emotions.	Teach your child about mindfulness and how to use it. There are several online sources just for kids.
Teach them how to recognize the signs in themselves that they are becoming overstimulated.	Give your child chances to be in charge and make decisions. This can be for an afternoon as they chose the activity, the restaurant, the movie, etc.	Encourage your child to express the why behind their emotions. "I am (emotion) because (reason).

Teens & Tweens

Have your child keep a gratitude journal.	Encourage your child to keep a diary or journal.	Encourage your child to find a hobby or group that interests them, such as music or art.
Listen to your teen talk without passing judgment. You may not understand all their choices, but that does not make their choices wrong. Let them know they can come to you at any time about anything.	Teach them the empty chair technique. Have them place an empty chair in front of them and have them visualize the person or thing that is causing them to feel an intense emotion and encourage them to talk as if the person or thing were present in the chair. Then they switch to the other chair and talk the way they think the person would respond. They can, of course, do this privately.	Teach your teen the concept of self-care. Encourage them to exercise or meditate. Take them to get their nails done or for a relaxing day at the pool or out for a round of golf. Provide them time to spend with their friends away from homework, chores, and other responsibilities.

Chapter 7 Quiz A

1. True or False: Social skills and emotional development form independently and need little to no parental guidance.

2. Which of the following are ways to support your School-aged child with their emotions? Select all that apply:
   a. Sing songs and nursery rhymes together
   b. Encourage them to journal or draw
   c. Use the empty chair technique
   d. Help them recognize the signs that they are becoming overstimulated

3. Which of the following are signs that your child may be anxious or overstimulated?
   e. They become clingy and whiny
   f. They ask a lot of questions about the event
   g. They are easily distracted and have trouble focusing
   h. All of the Above

4. What are the Three R's used to help you work with your child's anxiety?
   i. Recognize, Read, Respond
   j. Read, Relate, Respond,
   k. Recognize, Read, React
   l. Recognize, Relate, Respond

5. True or False: When your child has strong emotions, it is ok to comfort and support them without solving the problem for them.

QUIZ A ANSWER GUIDE

1: False. 2: B & D. 3: D. 4: A. 5: True

Manners

Another aspect of social skills is manners. Different cultures have different ideas about what constitutes good manners; for example, in many Asian cultures looking people directly in the eye is considered rude or disrespectful. In America, eye contact is considered a sign of respect. Therefore outside of common decency, this section aims not to tell you what constitutes good or polite manners but to guide you in teaching your child the importance of exhibiting those manners you deem important.

Many parents worry that their children will embarrass them in public with their poor manners or lack of social graces, so it's crucial to understand kids do not have an innate sense of manners; like all other social skills, manners must be taught.

One of the best ways to teach manners is to model them. If someone says hello to your child and your child is too shy to answer, instead of forcing them to say hello and putting them on the spot, do it for them, "Hello, Mr. Sabran! It's nice to see you too!" Then later, in a private moment, talk to your child and explain that while you understand being shy when someone says hello, the polite thing to do is say help back.

Apologies

Apologies are one of the most significant areas parents struggle with in manners.

Forcing your child to apologize for a mistake only places undue stress on them and makes them turn further inward. Since children need to be taught social skills and manners, they don't understand the reason for apologies. Forcing a four-year-old to apologize for hitting their bother is pointless because one, they are likely not sorry they did so, and two, they don't understand what an apology is or means.

Instead, model what an apology looks like, "I am sorry Jesse that Sasha hit you, that was not ok. Would you like a hug?" Another tactic is to teach your child to make amends for the mistake instead of a blanket apology policy. "Sasha, hitting Jesse is not ok; it hurts him. Jesse, what could Sasha do to make you feel better?" or "Ellie knocking down Marie's tower was unkind; you need to help her rebuild it now." Or "Marie, I'm sorry Ellie knocked down your tower. Would you like her to help you rebuild it?"

Repetition and Modeling

Depending on the child, they may need to give a lot of reminders to use their manners. This does not mean your child is rude or ungrateful; it just means their brain is having a more challenging time storing the information. If you hand your child something and are met with silence, prompt them with, "What do you say when someone gives you something?" or "I need to hear a thank you."

It is exhausting, but so much of parenting is teaching. Remember, the foundation is modeling. The more you show your child good manners, the more likely they are to emulate them. Your child learned to speak because you and other adults spoke to them. The same goes for manners.

It is also possible that your child may not know what to say in a situation, so provide them with the words. For example, if your three-year-old bumps into someone in line at the store, teach them on the spot that the words to say are "excuse me" or "I'm sorry."

When your child does use their manners or makes a positive choice, follow up with positive reinforcement. "I noticed you said you were sorry for pushing Jeremy on the playground; that was the right choice, and I'm proud of you!" Positive reinforcement is one of the best tools a parent has in their toolbox to encourage positive behavior in their child.

A final step in teaching your child manners is by ridding yourself of biases you may have, or if you're not able to rid yourself of the biases, restrain from commenting on them in front of your child. Just because you may disapprove of someone's choice of outfits, visible tattoos, the fact they are overweight, or a person in a non-traditional gender role does not give you license to make remarks about the person, especially in front of your child.

Your personal opinions are just that, personal and an opinion. Children are known to have no filter. If your child says, "Daddy, why is that lady so fat?" and it is likely they will make this or similar comments, the best thing for you to do is calmly say, "People come in all different shapes and sizes, and that is ok, but it is not nice to call someone fat, it will hurt their feelings."

Your Moral Code

Before you can teach your child manners, you need to understand what you consider to constitute good manners and temper that with realistic expectations for your child's age. Using a fork and knife while at the table is widely considered good manners in western culture, but you should not be expecting your six-year-old to sit perfectly at the table and never spill or drop anything.

Where does your idea of good manners stem from? Are they based on religious concepts, your culture, what your mother or father taught you or didn't teach you?

Take some time with the reflective questions below to consider what manners are important to you and why.

Reflective Questions

1. Were manners an important part of your household growing up?

_____

_____

_____

_____

_____

_____

2. Do you feel good manners are essential? Why or why not?

_____

_____

_____

_____

3. Where do you think your basis for what you believe to be appropriate manners comes from?

_____

_____

_____

_____

4. Do you model appropriate manners for your child? Where is there room for improvement?

_____

_____

_____

_____

5. What personal biases do you have that may make it difficult to exhibit good manners in some situations?

_____

_____

_____

_____

Making Friends

One social skill area your child may need assistance with is making friends. Some children are naturally more social and outgoing than others, and you've probably observed the same in adults. When children are young, most make friends easily. They play with anyone who is around regardless of race, gender, age, etc. As children age and prepare to enter school around five or six years old, they may become slightly more hesitant to play with someone they don't know, but they are still likely to play with both genders.

School-age children begin to adhere closely to their gender group. They are developing their concept of what it means to be a boy or a girl and may cling tightly to gender stereotypes even if you've raised them to believe that both boys and girls are equal. Statements like pink is for girls, and all boys like trucks will become common in the late preschool and early elementary school years. They will likely begin to play with people who share similar interests as them, for example, video games and baseball, or music and swimming, and may even find people that are different than them "weird."

While you cannot force your child to like someone else, it is important to teach them that friends do not have to be all the same. You can have a friend who loves ballet even if you find it boring and love skateboarding. Teaching them to respect another person's interests is an essential step in making friends as they age.

If your child struggles to make or maintain friendships, consider having them join a group sport or an activity like children's theater or a dance class based on their interests. Once children reach late elementary and early teen years, they are less likely to make new friends independently without some shared interest.

Teens & Friends

As your child enters the teen years, they begin exploring and experimenting with who they are. It is possible that you will begin to feel disconnected from your child and may even feel like a stranger has taken over your once adorable child's body. Be patient and open-minded. Think back to when you were a teen; you probably didn't see eye to eye with your parents on everything either.

As our teens gravitate further away from us and more towards their friendships, there is a natural desire to pull them back, but pulling too hard can have adverse effects. If you don't understand your child's choice of friends, invite them into your home to get to know them better. As long as your teen's friends aren't leading them down a destructive path, drugs, alcohol, skipping school, shoplifting, etc., do your best to embrace their choices.

Keep the lines of communication open with your teen; you can even say to them things like, "I don't understand why you enjoy being friends with Jemma. Can you explain it to me?" You may be surprised by their response.

The more autonomy you can give tour teens with their friendship choices, the less they are likely to rebel when it matters. Discuss peer pressure with your child, and provide them with phrases and tools to use if they feel like they are being pressured to do things they don't want to.

Tips to Help Your Teen with Peer Pressure

- Discuss values
- Discuss possible situations that may occur ahead of time
  - What should you do if....?
- Advise them to avoid situations where activities make them uncomfortable
  - Don't go to the party if they know people will be drinking, make other plans
- Advise them when faced with peer pressure to think about the positive and negative reasons and outcomes
- If they don't feel comfortable talking to you about a situation, encourage them to find another trusted adult such as a coach, teacher, aunt or uncle, etc.
- Come up with a code word if they need to call you and tell you they are in a bad situation but are afraid to say what is going on.

Peer Conflict & Bullying

On the flip side of friends are peer conflicts and bullying. Bullying is not a new issue, but it has taken on a never level of intensity with the introduction of electronic devices. Kids can be bullied 24/7 via the internet, chat rooms, text messages, and social media.

Bullying can happen at nearly any age, even as young as kindergarten; it is important to know the signs that your child may be being bullied.

Sings of Bullying

- Physical ailments such as stomach aches, headaches, or other unexplained physical complaints
- Unexplained cuts, bruises, scrapes
- Eating disorders like binge eating or not eating at all
- Difficulty sleeping or nightmares
- Changes in your child's grades
- Frequently "losing" possessions
- Loss of interest in favorite activities or hobbies, skipping practices or classes

If you suspect your child is being bullied, first try to speak with them. If they deny it and you still have suspicions call your child's school so the teachers can be put on the lookout for any possible bullying behavior.

If it is confirmed your child is the victim of bullying, schedule an appointment with a counselor or therapist for them to talk to.

Peer Conflict

Peer conflict is not the same as bullying, although it can be tricky to navigate as children get older. When young children have conflicts, parents and teachers are usually on the scene to help them solve the problem. Things like "Billy took my toy," "Miko pushed me," or "Ava said she's not my friend anymore" are commonplace in preschool and kindergarten. And while we know as adults, these are not life-ending events to a small child, they feel that way. These conflicts are also opportunities to teach our children how to resolve problems and solve more significant peer disagreements later in life.

Ways to Help Your Child Solve Peer Conflicts

Preschool – Kindergarten

- Include all children involved with the conflict in solving it
  - Allow each child the opportunity to describe what happened
- Ask for the children's input on how to solve the problem
- Bring their attention to how their actions or words may the other person or people feel
- Teach them strategies to handle the situation better next time

Elementary School

- Include all children involved with the conflict in solving it
  - Allow each child the opportunity to describe what happened
- Ask for the children's input on how to solve the problem
- Bring their attention to how their actions or words may the other person or people feel
- Teach them strategies to handle the situation better next time
- Encourage them to help solve the problem they created
- Discuss the importance of apologizing if they made a mistake or accepting a sincere apology from others
- Teach them how to use "I" Statements in place of blame.
  - "I feel (blank) when you (blank)
- Encourage them to listen to the other person without interrupting and to make eye contact

Tweens & Teens

- Include all children involved with the conflict in solving it
  - Allow each child the opportunity to describe what happened
- Ask for the children's input on how to solve the problem
- Bring their attention to how their actions or words may the other person or people feel
- Teach them strategies to handle the situation better next time
- Encourage them to help solve the problem they created
- Discuss the importance of apologizing if they made a mistake or accepting a sincere apology from others
- Teach them how to use "I" Statements in place of blame.
  - "I feel (blank) when you (blank)
- Encourage them to listen to the other person without interrupting and to make eye contact
- Discuss compromise and flexibility
- Brainstorm solutions with them
- Teach them appropriate tools for handling strong emotions

Conversation Starters to Use with Older Children, Tweens, and Teens

- Is there anything you want or need to talk to me about?
- Who did you eat lunch with today?
- Tell me about rehearsal (practice, chess club, art class, etc.)
- Who have you been hanging out with lately?
- You seem quiet lately. Is there anything you want to tell me?
- What's your favorite song right now? Can I listen?
- I notice you've been hanging out with (Sonia) a lot lately; what do you guys do together? Would she like to come over for dinner one night?
- Do you have any new interests or hobbies?

Age-Appropriate Social Skills

Ages 3-6

Begin playing with peers, more social interactions

Makes first "real" friend(s) that they look forward to seeing

Easily gets over peer conflicts, does not hold grudges

Needs adult support to solve most peer conflicts

Difficulty delaying gratification, taking turns (I want it now!)

Able to hold conversations of 3+ exchanges

Makes new friends easily

Begins to understand the concept of empathy (becomes less egocentric

Begins to be able to express wants, needs, and emotions

Ages 6-10

Will develop and play elaborate make-believe games

Enjoys group games, board games, card games, etc.

Usually quickly gets over peer conflicts, does not hold grudges

May need adult help to solve peer conflicts

Able to take turns with increasing ability

Able to hold lengthy conversations, especially on topics that interest them

Makes new friends easily

Able to see situations from another person's point of view

Tends to play with friends of the same gender

May seek out friends with similar interests

Increasingly able to express emotions, wants, and needs

Ages 10-13

Typically enjoys team and group games and activities

May have "fights" with friends that last several days, usually they resolve themselves

Interest in hanging out with friends more

The majority of their friends will still be of the same gender

May have difficulty making new friends

Will likely seek out friends with similar interests

May talk less to parents seem more withdrawn

May begin to show an interest in dating or having a "boyfriend" or "girlfriend" as puberty begins

Ages 13-17

Typically enjoys team and group games and activities .

May completely change friend group or stop being friends with people as they grow and change interests

Seeking independence in time with friends, fewer "rules" about where they go

Interest in going to parties, weekends away with friends' family

May begin to have friends of the opposite gender again

May have difficulty making new friends

Will likely seek out friends with similar interests

May talk less to parents seem more withdrawn

Will likely begin dating if parents allow

Begin to mature mentally, able to hold their own conversing on adult topics

Chapter Eight
Co-Parenting

Respecting the Other Parent

Whether you are co-parenting with your child's biological parent and your spouse, step-parent, grandparent, an ex whom you can't stand, or a parent who only sees your child a few times a year, it is crucial for your child's well-being that you show respect to one another.

Saying negative comments about the other parent in front of your child is damaging to your child's mental health. Your child is not involved in any disagreement you may have had or currently have with their other parent. They still love that parent and look up to them, and hearing negative comments confuses and hurts them. Your child should never feel that their loyalty has to be divided or that they have to choose one parent over the other.

Save your venting for your trusted friends and family members out of the earshot of your children. If you feel you have no one to talk to about concerns or frustrations, join an online support group for single parents or whatever situation fits your needs best.

Any conversations that affect how you and your co-parent will be handling situations with your child should be discussed in private. Fundamental parenting decisions such as bedtimes, routines, discipline should be discussed and agreed upon and followed in the same way by both parents.

Even parents in the same home are likely to have disagreements about handling certain situations, but the best thing you can do for your child is to present a united front. Remember, when parents fight, it is the children who suffer.

If needed, to keep tempers in check, schedule to have serious conversations in a public or neutral setting which is likely to help keep tempers down and the conversation focused.

This doesn't mean that you can never disagree in front of your children. In fact, when children see adults have a disagreement and come to an amicable solution, it models for them that it is ok to disagree. However, those discussions should never be about the children.

Reflective Questions

1. What is your current co-parent situation?
2. What struggles do you find in your current co-parenting situation?
3. What is a recent parenting situation you and your co-parent have disagreed on lately?
4. What are one or two areas in your current co-parenting situation you'd like to see improved?

Basic Parenting Rights

The details of any custody agreement you have will affect your or your co-parent's parental rights but in general fundamental parental rights include:

- ✓ Right to physical custody, which means reasonable visitation
- ✓ Right to legal custody, the ability to make major decisions
  - Religion
  - Education
  - Medical Treatments
- ✓ Right to pass property to a child via gift or inheritance
- ✓ Right to a child's earnings and to inherit from a child in case of death

These parental rights pertain to any adult who is the legal parent or guardian of a child, whether through adoption, court order, or biologically listed as the parent on the child's birth certificate. Adoption is the only way for a non-biological parent to obtain access to all of these parental rights.

It is possible that while custody cases and divorce proceedings are going on, a judge may make temporary decisions that affect one or both parents' parental rights. These decisions may affect visitation rights, custody, and child support.

If you are going through a divorce or legal separation, it is vital that you seek out legal counsel to ensure you have access to all the rights you are entitled to and wish to maintain.

Parents also have legal responsibilities to their children, meeting their child's basic needs for food, clothing, housing, medical care, and education.

A child is anyone under the age of 18. All children have these rights regardless of race, gender, religion, language spoken, or abilities.

Parents are expected to make decisions with the best interest of their children in mind. The government is responsible for ensuring children have access to their basic rights and needs and that children are protected and looked after by their parents.

For more information on the child's rights as outline by the Convention on the Rights of the Child, you can visit Unicef.org.

Chapter 8 Quiz A

1. Which of the following are not a basic right of a child as outlined by the Convention on the Rights of the Child?
   a. Food
   b. Housing
   c. Medical Attention
   d. Toys
2. True or False: A judge may change visitation rights during a custody battle.
3. True or False: A parent should make decisions with the best interest of their child in mind.
4. True or False: You should never disagree in front of your child.
5. True or False: Saying negative and hurtful comments about your child's other parent can cause mental damage to your child.
6. Which of the following is the best way to have a serious conversation about your child with your co-parent?
   a. In front of your child because they should be involved in all decisions about their well-being
   b. In private in a calm, neutral setting.
   c. In a busy, crowded restaurant or bar.
   d. Over the phone.
7. True or False: All parents have the same rights to their children regardless of parental legal status.
8. True or False: Respect is vital when co-parenting.

QUIZ A ANSWER GUIDE

1: D. 2: True. 3: True. 4: False. 5: True. 6: B. 7: False 8: True.

Handling Conflicts

Co-parenting is an emotional roller coaster. Of course, you want what is best for your child, but you may also be dealing with someone you used to have a relationship with; perhaps you were married or in a long-term relationship. Even if you are parenting with your spouse, whom you are still in love with, there are bound to be disagreements and tension from time to time.

Here are some basic ground rules when attempting to handle conflict and disagreements with a co-parent.

- Allow the past to stay in the past. Disagreements about past hurt in the relationship should not come up when discussing parenting. Do not allow your feelings about the other person as a partner to influence your decisions on their parenting. Many people are horrible spouses but great parents. The exception to this rule is if things from the past affected the safety or well-being of your child.

- Don't be afraid of conflict. That is often easier said than done, but it is crucial to face disagreements head-on; otherwise, resentment may grow deeper. Skirting around the edges of conflict can sometimes make the other person more suspicious or irritated.

- Never assume someone's meaning or intentions; always seek clarification if you are unsure. Making assumptions leads to confusion and possibly further clarification. This is a good rule in any situation; if the details are important, make sure you understand them.

- Take the time to formulate a response. If you need more than the present, let them know you need to think about it, and you will respond as soon as you've had a chance to think it through. Even if you can answer right then and there, slow down and take a few extra seconds to formulate your thoughts before responding.

- Be aware of your word choice and tone of voice. Saying, "I am not comfortable with her going on an overnight trip with a friend yet; I am not sure she's ready for that," is much different than saying, "Are you crazy? There is no way she can handle that; what a stupid idea!" Both statements say you don't like the idea, but one is much more likely to be received calmly than the other.

- It's not always about winning the argument; there will be times you have to concede or compromise. Be careful you don't exhaust yourself fighting just to win over something that does not mean a lot to you. Save those battles for the big things.

- Your child comes first. Repeat and remember this; your child comes first. No matter your feelings for the other person, what is best for your child must always come first.

Suppose you and your co-parent are not able to be civil to one another or have productive conversations. In that case, you may need to involve a mediator to help you solve issues concerning parenting. A mediator needs to be a non-biased person who is not connected to either one of you personally, so your best friend or her mother will not work.

You can hire a professional mediator to help you solve problems, or you may be able to use a relationship or family therapist as well to help solve problems.

Reflective Questions

1. Do you trust your co-parent with your child? Why or why not?
2. Do you have any past hurts you need to work through to have a productive relationship with your co-parent?
3. Have you ever used a mediator or therapist? Would you consider using one? Why or why not?

Chapter 8 Quiz B

1. True to False: To avoid conflict, you should just assume what the other person is saying and not upset them with many questions.
2. True or False: When handling conflict, it is advisable to keep the past in the past, the exception being if a past action by the other person has affected the health or safety of your child.
3. True or False: Co-parenting, even with a spouse or partner you love, is still likely to have conflict and disagreements.
4. True or False: A family therapist or a mediator is an option if you and your co-parent have difficulty having conversations.
5. True or False: Winning arguments over what you think is best for your child is the most important thing.

QUIZ B ANSWER GUIDE

1: False. 2: True. 3: True. 4: True. 5: False.

Helping Your Child with Transitions

If you are in a co-parenting situation where your children have to transition from one household to another, those transitions can be tough on your children. Even if you have an amicable and friendly relationship with your co-parent, moving back and forth requires frequent transitions for your child.

All people enjoy routine. Routine is predictable, and it means you know what is coming next. Constant changes are upsetting to even adults, but they can be even more upsetting to children because children cannot regulate their emotions as fluently as adults.

Setting up a predictable schedule for your children is the first step in easing transitions. They can begin to learn to anticipate the schedule, even if it means shuffling back and forth between homes.

You can use a picture schedule or calendar to help children learn their schedules. You can use a specific picture or symbol to represent each parent's house.

On the day of the transition, prepare your child by reminding them earlier in the day that they will be going to "mom's" house tonight. Then about an hour before giving them another reminder. Follow that up about 10 minutes before they are expected to leave. This way, there are no surprises when it is time to leave.

It would help if you had all their things packed and ready to go ahead of time. If your child needs to move things back and forth, include them in the process of getting ready for the transition. If your child stays for shorter periods, a weekend, or just a few nights a week, purchase them a special "go bag" like a backpack they can always have with them.

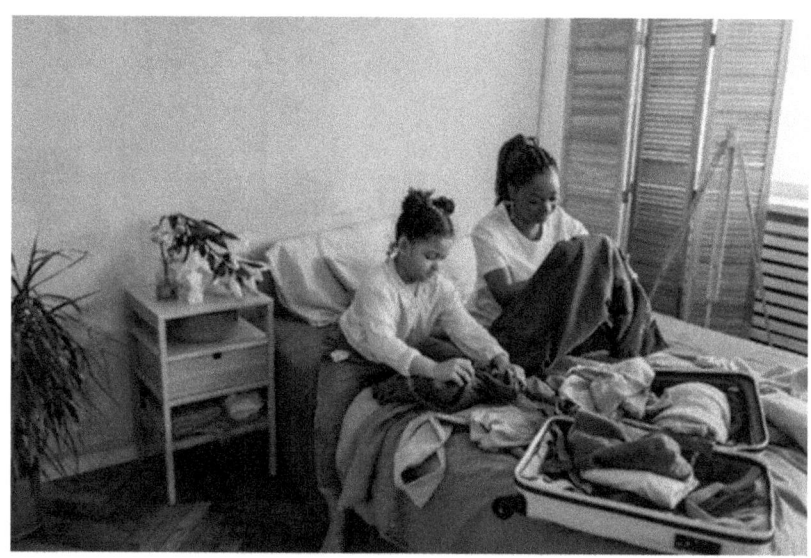

If your co-parent is unreliable and has let your child down in the past by now showing up when scheduled, it may be better not to give reminders because your risk upsetting your child if their other parent is a no-show. If your child asks, do not make promises on behalf of their other parent, but remain positive with phrases like, "I'm sure he'll be here if he can," or "I know she's trying to get here." Do not bad mouth the other parents. If the other parent is unreliable, consider having your child's things packed and ready to go out of the to be prepared.

Keep your child engaged with another fun activity while waiting for their parent to show up to keep them distracted and not worried about whether or not they will be there.

Communication with your co-parent about your child's schedule is key. Even if they are someone you usually would never talk to again, you have to put your child first. This may mean being the "bigger person" from time to time. It may feel unfair and anger you if you are playing by the rules of respectful communication and they aren't, but remember you are doing more harm than good if you start arguing and bad-mouthing your co-parent. Keeping an open and respectful line of communication going means there is less likely to be surprises.

When parents are kind and civil to one another and avoid speaking negatively about or to one another, it helps your child remain calm and confident. Consider having a picture of your co-parent in your home, or at least in your child's bedroom.

Schedules and routines such as getting ready for school in the morning or bedtime should be the same at both homes. Changes in schedules between homes can confuse your child because they don't know what to expect. By maintaining consistent schedules, you will avoid comments like, "Well, at Dad's house we….".

If your child is missing their other parent, allow them to communicate with them regularly, whether over facetime or on the phone. Being allowed to reach out to the parent, they're missing can help ease transition stress for your child.

Transition objects can also be helpful if your child has difficulty going back and forth between homes. Transition objects can be a stuffed animal, a photo album, or a special blanket.

Reflective Questions

1. Does your child have a consistent schedule between your home and your co-parents?
2. Can you rely on your co-parent to consistently pick up your child when they are scheduled? Why or why not?
3. If you cannot rely on your co-parent to pick up or spend time with your child regularly, what are some distractions and coping mechanisms you can use to help your child?
4. What is communication like with your co-parent? What could you do to improve it?

Blended Families

Blended families are more and more common in modern society, and that is a great thing; however, blending families can cause a lot of stress as you try to figure out everyone's role in your new situation.

Before you and your new partner move in together or marry, it is essential to discuss how you will handle parenting situations ahead of time. Much of that will be determined by the children's ages, the amount of time they spend at your home, and if you have children together. Making those decisions ahead of time will reduce any possible resentment your child may feel towards your new spouse.

It is also a good idea to consider and involve your co-parent in the discussion at some point because, in the end, your new spouse's decisions and parenting will affect their child. At the very least, no major decision regarding your child should be decided without your child's other parent's input, even if the final decision falls to you.

You must avoid ultimatums. Neither your new spouse nor your children should put you in a situation where you are asked to choose between one or the other. If either puts you in this position, be firm and let them know you will not tolerate ultimatums.

Children need to feel loved, safe, and secure. Creating an open and honest environment where your children can discuss their feelings about the situation will help them with the new situation.

Children under the age of ten are likely to adjust more quickly to a blended family than teens, but they may also be more competitive for their parent's attention. Find time every day to spend with your child as they adjust. You also need to set aside special time with your spouse regularly.

Expect that there may be some behavioral problems as your child works out their emotions and where they fit into the new family. Your child may direct anger at your spouse, or they may turn inward. If you are concerned about your child's adjustment, consider having them talk to a therapist to ease the transition.

Conclusion

Congratulations! You have reached the end of the parenting manual. You should be proud of all the work you put into learning about parenting and child development. Parenting is, without a doubt, the most challenging job you will ever have, and it comes with the fewest instructions.

Not this book nor any other can guarantee smooth parenting, but the more you learn, the easier the path will be, and this book is a step in the right direction.

If you took this manual seriously, answered the reflective questions truthfully and with thought, you will likely gain more out of this than if you passively read through.

This manual can be returned to as you face different parenting struggles through the years. Revisit the questions and quizzes over time and reflect on how your answers have changed as you grow as a parent and your child grows and develops.

Parenting and raising a child are fluid, so be prepared for constant changes, ups, downs, and everything in between. No matter what happens, when in doubt, love your child and put them first.

Remember you are your child's first protector, caregiver, and teacher. What you model for them is what they will learn and take out into the world. Take time to learn about yourself, what is important to you and what knowledge and guidance you wish to pass down to your children.

No person is perfect, and there is no such thing as the perfect parent. The perfect parent is the one who shows up every day, who puts their child's needs first, and who loves their child unconditionally.